HARMONY IN HORSEMANSHIP

This book is intended to provide a complete course for both horse and rider in the art of show jumping, and is written by an acknowledged expert on the subject. The author has been a member of the British Olympic jumping team and also trained the Olympic gold medal winning team of 1952.

After describing his own riding background, Colonel Talbot-Ponsonby looks at the history of show jumping and the situation of the sport to-day, with reference to such topical points as the influence of television and the effect of the Olympic Games every fourth year. Later chapters describe the various types of obstacle facing the show jumper, and explain how each is best tackled. A method of training young horses is given, taking them right up to the show ring, and the rider is instructed in the whole technique of competition jumping, from choosing a saddle to the inspection of the course, and the actual jumping of the round.

The book is illustrated with many fine photographs by Rex Coleman, and there are diagrams to clarify technical points. The whole subject of show jumping is studied in great detail, although much of the book's teaching is not solely confined to the show ring, for, as the author says: 'I know that the suggestions I have made for educating horses on the flat and over fences are applicable to any horse that is to jump first or last in the hunting field, and many of the suggestions can be beneficial to the training of steeplechasers.'

Lieut.-Colonel
J. A. Talbot-Ponsonby

Jack Talbot-Ponsonby has been connected with horses all his life. He was born in 1907 in County Kildare, his father being Master of the Kildare Hounds from 1911 to 1921. He was educated at Harrow and the Royal Military College, Sandhurst, and was gazetted in 1927 to a well-known cavalry regiment, the 7th Queen's Own Hussars. He became Regimental Equitation Officer in 1932 and was later an Instructor at the Equitation School, Weedon, until he retired from the Army in 1938, to school horses in Northamptonshire.

He returned when war broke out in 1939 and commanded, in succession, a squadron of the Northamptonshire Yeomanry, the 1st/6th Lancashire Fusilier Tank Battalion, and the 59th Reconnaissance Regiment.

Harmony in Horsemanship

by

Lieut.-Colonel J. A. Talbot-Ponsonby

London
J. A. Allen & Co. Ltd.

First published in 1964 by
Country Life Limited
Reprinted 1972, 1976 by
J. A. Allen & Co. Ltd.
1 Lower Grosvenor Place
London SW1W 0EL

SBN 85131 169 5

Printed in Great Britain by
Lewis Reprints Ltd.
member of Brown Knight & Truscott Group
London and Tonbridge

Foreword

by Brigadier P. E. Bowden-Smith, c.b.e.

The writer of this book has a vast amount of experience and tremendous records behind him. Quite early in his show jumping career he became the first man to win the King George V Trophy at the Royal International Horse Show three times— in 1930 and 1932 on a mare called Chelsea, and in 1934 on a mare called Best Girl. He thereby won the trophy outright, but generously handed it back to the Royal International Horse Show for perpetual competition. He also rode in the British Team in many countries, especially in the U.S.A. and Canada. He jumped at Boston, New York, Toronto, Dublin (when he was in the first British Team to win the Aga Khan Cup), at the Berlin Olympic Games, and at many other places. His name has been conncected with many good horses, among them Irish Eagle, Standard, Blue Dun, Big Sweep, Kineton, and his two King's Cup winners.

All this proves, without any assurances from me, that he knows what he is writing about. He deals with everything in great detail, but his book is none the less interesting, pleasantly written and easy to understand. I feel that many who read this book will be filled with a desire to improve their riding. Having known the author intimately since he first began jumping, not only as a very high class trainer of horses and their riders, but also as a trainer of soldiers, I am well acquainted with his thoroughness, and the time and trouble he always gave to his programmes. Never was any of his trainees asked to run before he or she could walk, and in that lies the secret of his many successes. I hope that this book will be yet another.

To my wife, Daphne, who shares
my love for horses

Contents

Illustrations

PHOTOGRAPHS

9

DIAGRAMS IN TEXT

With the exception of Plates 1, 2, 11 and 28, all photographs were taken by Rex Coleman, Baron Studios

Part One

CONSIDERATIONS AFFECTING THE WHOLE
PERFORMANCE

My Own Background

Evolution of Riding Methods 1900–39

Post-war Show Jumping 1945–63

Present-day Requirements for Horse and Rider

Some Technical Problems Set for Horse and Rider

CHAPTER ONE

My Own Background

A background can dominate a whole life, and this is certainly so in my case. My first recollections were of things connected with horses and hounds. I suppose that this is hardly surprising since my father was a fox-hunting devotee, to the extent of being almost a fanatic, and was equally knowledgeable on the subject of both horses and hounds, and also because I spent the first fourteen years of my life in Ireland where, certainly in those days, ordinary life in the country revolved around them. With Irish blood in my veins, perhaps I am biased, but to me the Emerald Isle will always mean horses and hounds, and anything else that happens there will always seem to me to be entirely subsidiary to these two.

My father was a regular soldier, but having found himself stationed at Newbridge, County Kildare, it did not take long before his natural love of hunting got the better of his professional ambitions. He left the Army just before I was born, and settled down to live in a charming house on the River Liffey, near the small village of Kilcullen. After several seasons hunting the New-bridge beagles he became Master and Huntsman of the Kildare Hounds in 1911, a post he held until 1921, when to my sorrow, and I know to his also, we left Ireland and moved to Devonshire, a county he chose because it provided banks to be ridden over!

I certainly make no pretension to having been even remotely an infant prodigy on a horse. In fact my first recollection of real hunting, on a three-year-old cob when I was eight years old, is one of very considerable apprehension. However, having gone through a period when Tommy the cob was virtually master of the situation, I found that his latent intelligence would look after the two of us, that the whole thing was magnificent fun, and that, as I had so often heard my father say, 'No colour like red, no sport like hunting'.

My sister (three years my senior and a great one to go) and I were fortunate indeed to have the stud groom, Willie Deakin, as our constant guide and philosopher. Willie, brought to Ireland by my father as a young man, was a great character, a wonderful companion, and a top class horseman; and his knowledge of animal life in general was profound. My own love of animals is a natural one, but any understanding I may have of their thoughts and actions is owed in large measure to Willie's always cheerful and encouraging promptings. Although today his technical approach to riding might not be considered to be quite up to date, or particularly penetrating, his results with young horses were always good. He usually had a young one of his own to break, make and sell. When it was ready for sale I was sometimes given a ride on it—hunting, on the theory, I suppose, that if a boy of ten or eleven could ride it across Kildare there could not be much wrong with it! One of Willie's jobs was to keep an eye on my sister and me when out hunting; not an easy job, as of course we did everything we could to slip him. One day at the end of a good hunt my father, noticing Willie's absence, asked us what had become of him. My sister Molly blithely replied: 'Oh, he's in a ditch; but he's all right—you can't kill old Willie!'

Ireland is an unpredictable, and in many ways a sad country, and her history has been one of upheaval, and often tragedy. The Irish countryside is beautiful and, to a foreigner, the complete silence is striking. Her people have usually been 'agin any form of government'; and sometimes the constant faint rumblings have developed into violent explosions, but we must hope that the troubles of 1916, and those of 1920 and 1921, may never be repeated. When we were children, their severity, pathos, and cruelty passed over our heads. They were just added excitement to our already full lives. But no sort of trouble was allowed to stop fox-hunting. Ominous knocks on the door at night did not herald fire and destruction for us, but only that some bridge needed blowing up, and that a car magneto was wanted to carry out the job. By morning another magneto had appeared, and my father could still get to the meet to display the sport that was expected of him. Unpredictable as Ireland is, her charm will never fade.

I continued to ride and hunt in the school holidays, and during my time as a cadet at the Royal Military College, Sandhurst, kept a horse of my own, in addition to riding twice a week as a normal part of the curriculum. It was here that I had my first introduction to show jumping. Colonel Joe Dudgeon was in charge of equitation, and being a keen jumping rider himself he encouraged it among cadets in inter-company competitions. Although opportunities were few, I realised that there was a great deal to show jumping, and that as a sport it held definite attractions. On being commissioned to the 7th Queen's Own Hussars in January, 1927, it came as no surprise to me to find that jumping was a favourite sport among the best horsemen of non-commissioned rank, but it was puzzling that few officers practised it. I discovered, however, that they rather looked down on it; polo was their recognised summer sport. Nevertheless, I soon found myself drawn into show jumping. When the 12th Lancers were mechanised in 1926 their horses were distributed among regiments stationed in England. One of them, an aged brown mare, Chelsea, was allotted to the 7th Hussars and, having something of a reputation as a jumper, was quickly snapped up by our Rough Riding Sergeant-major, Tom Wallis, himself a keen show jumping rider. Chelsea obviously deserved her reputation, and it became Wallis's ambition for her to jump at the International Horse Show, Olympia. As an N.C.O. he was ineligible to ride there, but he searched among the young officers, and chose me. With more than considerable trepidation, but having a very healthy respect for such an important figure as the S.S.M.R.I., I agreed to enter, and at Olympia in 1928 I embarked on international show jumping. (Plate 1.)

Chelsea, in addition to being a top class jumper, winning the King George V Gold Cup at Olympia in 1930 and 1932, was the kindest, friendliest, and most willing horse I have ever had the pleasure of riding. She taught me a very great deal. In 1929 I was fortunate in being sent on a ten months' course at the Equitation School, Weedon, in Northamptonshire. Cavalry and Royal Artillery regiments had to be equipped with both officer and N.C.O. riding instructors, and these were trained at the school. Weedon was not an establishment that offered any specialised branch of riding. Its aims were to produce instructors who were good all-round horsemen, with a knowledge of what a trained horse should be, with practical experience in schooling young ones, and with the ability to impart their knowledge to others. With a very mixed bag of students on each course the school programme could not include any particular aspect of riding. However, the passing out school test incorporated all movements up to, and including, the change at the canter, the last before High School work is introduced; and the basic factors in show jumping were taught and practised. This was not an easy task as only a very few of the horses had any pretensions to being real show jumpers. Cross-country work was also done, both on green and experienced horses. Individuals, however, worked at different subjects that particularly appealed to them. R.Q.M.S., now Major Jim Russell, studied the finer points of competitive dressage, in addition to training Best Girl, the mare I rode when I won the King's Cup for the third time in 1934 (Plate 2), and several of us tried to understand and follow the changing trends in show jumping technique, with expert help and cheerful encouragement from Col. 'Bogey' Bowden-Smith. On my return to Weedon in 1935 as an instructor for three years I had every opportunity for this.

It is now the custom to look down on Weedon and its teachings, which I suppose happens to any instructional institution that has been closed for many years. During its active life Weedon progressed with the times, although slowly, but since its demise its teachings have of necessity remained dormant. While still in its heyday Weedon came in for some possibly rather envious criticism! The fact that the instructors and student officers were regularly to be seen hunting with the Pytchley, Grafton, Bicester and Warwickshire, drew the very natural comment that the Weedon officers did little but enjoy themselves, although some members of the field were sometimes grateful for a hole in a thick bullfinch! In fact fox-hunting was a part of the curriculum. Initiative, quick decisions, an eye for the country, making the best of the existing situation—all these were part of a cavalryman's equipment, and during the 'thirties the cavalry were still horsed. From our point of view we had the privilege of watching the great huntsmen of that era; Frank Freeman and Stanley Barker of the Pytchley, Will Pope of the Grafton, Clarence Johnson of the Bicester, George Gilson of the Warwickshire, and sometimes Peaker of the Fernie. When lucky enough to be riding 'The old one, the tried one, the horse of my heart', I found it not so difficult to enjoy to the full Will Ogilvie's sentiments:

1. 'Chelsea', winner of the King George V Gold Cup at Olympia in 1930 and 1932, jumping at the Dublin Horse Show of 1930.

2. 'Best Girl', on whom I won the King George V Gold Cup for the third time at Olympia in 1934, and so outright. (Photograph: W. W. Rouch)

3. Lieut.-Colonel Dan Corry, a member of the famous Irish Free State jumping team of the 'thirties, still representing his country at Rotterdam in 1958.

'*But level as far as eye can see
like smooth green tinted glass,
a battle ground for bravery,
is spread the English grass.*'

The 'thirties were gay and sparkling. There seemed little to
worry about, and the young men of the day set out to work and
play to the best possible advantage. As a professional soldier,
although one with rather a single-track mind, the ominous word
'war' came into my mind at that time, only to be brushed rapidly
aside until I visited Berlin in 1936 to jump in the Olympic Games.
A glimpse of Hitler and his thugs in that doomed city convinced
me that war was inevitable, but in England the shadows grew
dim again. During the summer I show jumped, as and when
opportunity came, riding Weedon or Regimental troop horses,
and I also played some adventurous polo. Every year at Olympia
I watched the steady growth of the famous Irish Free State
team (Plate 3), under the guidance of that great instructor,
Paul Rodzianko, himself a King's Cup winner when leading the
Russian team in 1912, and all the time envying them their
string of quality horses. I sat and marvelled at Captain Xavier
Bizard, the French ace, and listened to the nostalgic strains of the
Gold and Silver Waltz, which introduced the cantering movements in the Cadre Noir's superb display. Gay, flower-decked
Olympia, with its intimate holiday atmosphere, was one of the
highlights of the London season. One felt one could not miss it,
even at the thought of those great doors closing behind you,
leaving you alone to your fate on a young army horse!

Trips to Dublin, and on two occasions to the U.S.A. and
Canada, were great adventures in those days, but without government support or any other source of economic aid regular foreign
tours were not practicable. Such tours as did take place were
always great fun, of very high instructional value, and invariably
they had their moments of humour. In 1930 we were the first
British officers to set foot in Dublin after the 'troubles'. Our
blue patrol uniforms were not generally recognised, and I was
twice asked if I was a German! But the climax came in the parade
for the Aga Khan or Nations Cup. The Swiss team, a very good
one, was there, and rode in to the strains of the Swiss national
anthem, identical except for one note in the middle to 'God Save

B

the King'. At once half the audience began to sing the King, while
the other half 'clocked' them with the nearest available weapon!
Soon after peace had been restored we came in, again to the
strains of 'God Save the King'. A second chance of a really good
free-for-all could not be missed, and they were 'at it' again. A
splendid sight from inside the arena rail!

I learned a great deal from watching the accepted masters.
The outstanding teams were the Irish and Germans, with the
French always there or thereabouts, and the Dutch, Swiss and
Poles well up to the front. As international teams were confined
to military officers I saw no continental civilians. All good things,
alas, come to an end. In 1938 my tour of duty as instructor at
Weedon expired. By then my regiment was motoring round
Cairo in tanks, and I decided to resign my commission; I sent in
my papers, not without difficulty as this had never before
happened at Weedon, and set up on my own in the Pytchley
country taking horses in to school, an undertaking that my
Colonel described as 'unbefitting to an officer and a gentleman'!

My year as a civilian horse persuader, a term I prefer to that of
rough rider, was valuable to me in two ways. Trade was good and
therefore remunerative, and the many horses I rode, the majority
with some fault to adjust, helped me to make a quick assessment
of their respective situations, and to work out a plan to set matters
to rights. This has since held me in very good stead. But the clouds
of war descended on Europe, and by the end of August, 1939, I
was again in uniform, wearing my jodhpurs as a final act of
defiance against machinery in general!

This is no place to write of war. Indeed I would not presume
to usurp any small gap in a library shelf for the subject; such space
must always be kept for the Generals' diaries. It is enough to say
that I could not agree more with anything than with the state-
ment that 'War consists of long periods of intense boredom, in-
terspersed with short periods of intense fear'. I rode when I could,
at one time directing tank training from my favourite hunter's
back. Tanks held no terrors for him, but infantry walking in line
frightened him to death. And I did have an excellent five mile
point with my squadron of Northamptonshire Yeomanry tanks
across the cream of the Whaddon Chase country, being holload
across the first road by George Gilson, the Warwickshire huntsman. The fact that I survived has always astonished me, but in

the autumn of 1945 I was once more a civilian in my old job, trying to persuade all sorts of horses to carry their owners satisfactorily. Soon my interests broadened to include tuition to show jumping riders, and in 1949 I was given my first assignment as part-time trainer to the British jumping team, a job I continued with at intervals until the end of 1960. So much then for my background. Once real interest in horses has been awakened, nothing will ever damp it. Their movements, their reflexes, their behaviour and their mental set-up, are a constant source of discussion and discovery. The more one knows about them the more one realises how small that knowledge is. Most people are inquisitive, and a horseman needs to be one of their number. I think the best of them are those who remember that 'Happy is the man who rides for his own pleasure, and not to astonish others'.

PART ONE

CHAPTER TWO

Evolution of Riding Methods 1900-39

It is remarkable that horse show jumping, or show jumping as we know it, is a twentieth century contribution to riding. The first International Competition took place at Olympia in London in 1907, and the Stockholm Olympic Games of 1912 marked the inauguration of Equestrian Events as regular items in the games programme. Before 1900 jumping does not seem to have been of any great technical interest. In England, the home of fox-hunting, the process of field enclosure began in the reign of Queen Elizabeth I, but was not finished until the middle of the nineteenth century. By that date jumping fences of all types in the hunting field had become, to the majority of followers of the chase, one of the main reasons for going fox-hunting, and to some indeed the only one! The first Grand National Steeplechase was run at Aintree in 1839, but there is no evidence that jumping, and the preparation for the jump, had been studied as an important part of riding. None of the books on equitation of that period made more than a passing reference to jumping, so one must assume that the great cross-country riders of the day instinctively understood the meaning of balance and free forward riding. Had they not, it would surely have been impossible for them to cross the very formidable obstacles in the English countryside with any degree of safety, obstacles which, from all accounts, would make many of the present-day top-liners think twice! But, first-class horsemen as they indubitably were, the technicalities connected with the mechanics of the jump both for horse and rider were of no very great moment to them; extreme accuracy was not essential for the purpose of landing safely in the next field.

The advent of competitive horse show jumping put a new complexion on the matter. Accuracy throughout the whole performance at once became of paramount importance for this type of sport; and detailed methods of the ways and means of producing such accuracy began to warrant close study. Nevertheless, the hazards of fox-hunting, certainly before the use of barbed wire, provided their own valuable lessons; and today, when the difficulties and frustrations met with when riding across the average hunting country have vastly increased, the same lessons, to a lesser extent, are still there to be learned, lessons which are all of inestimable value to those interested in any form of competitive jumping. When hounds really settle to run, it is quick thinking, split-second decisions, and instantaneous action to implement them, that will keep the flying pack in sight. The awkward dilemmas and tricky situations in which horses and riders find themselves when negotiating a varied assortment of obstacles help them both to find their way out of tight corners, to keep their heads when disaster seems imminent, and generally to take the rough with the smooth. It might well be illuminating to see the best horsemen of the last half of the nineteenth century facing the problems of present-day competitive jumping, and I feel that it is a thousand pities that the number of ardent fox-hunters among the ranks of modern show jumping and three-day event riders can be counted on the fingers of two hands.

Until 1900 the only international type of educated or reasoned riding was manège riding as applicable to the High School, and no serious thought had been given to its development for purposes of jumping, or fast cross-country work. At the turn of the century, however, an Italian, Capt. Federico Caprilli, began to work on a completely new method of cavalry riding. His method was based on observation of the natural mechanics of the horse's movements, and the rider's reactions to them. His conclusions were not confined to the jump itself, but were drawn also from a study of the horse's actions and impulses on the flat between jumps, with particular reference to the last few strides before take-off. Having decided that nature must know the best answer to the horse's problems in relation to jumping, he evolved a position for the rider to adopt on the horse's back from which it would be certain that he could allow nature to have its way, and at the same time maintain control. Perhaps Caprilli's most revolutionary theories were that the rider should never be entirely seated in the saddle, to the extent that, if the back of the saddle were to be cut off, he would not notice its absence, and that, to lighten the horse's load, weight should be placed on the horse's forehand, leaving the propelling apparatus, the loins and quarters, free. In short he advocated forward riding at all times and at all paces. He maintained that a rider should not interfere with a horse's general freedom or with his instinctive preparation for a jump, and was insistent that a horse's eye should be developed so that he would acquire the ability to choose with precision the right moment to take off.

These tenets of Caprilli's teaching indicated clearly that he considered it should be *the horse's* prerogative to decide upon stride arrangements during the ultimate part of the approach to a jump, and also upon the moment of take-off. Apart from the fact that the technicalities of jumping had, until then, never seriously been studied, Caprilli's methods were considered to be radical indeed, and it was some years before they were generally adopted in the Italian Cavalry. Gradually, however, his doctrines became widely known and were assimilated by such countries as Russia, U.S.A., Switzerland, Poland, Portugal and Sweden. It should be remembered that at the time that Caprilli evolved his new and excellent methods the size and difficulty of fences presented for competitive jumping events did not bear comparison with those of today.

From its inception until the second World War participants in international show jumping were military officers. Civilians took part in national competitions in some countries, but generally the new sport was a military perquisite which, in most instances, was encouraged and subsidised by governments for national prestige, horse trade, or the fostering of friendly international relations. As show jumping got under way, it fell to the cavalry schools of the world to study, improve, and perfect their systems for coping with show jumping problems. In England little or no thought was given to the subject until after the first World War, although, as I have mentioned, an annual horse show, comprising international jumping, was held at Olympia from 1907. In 1922 a Military Equitation School was opened at Weedon, as successor to the Netheravon Cavalry School, its rôle being to train regimental instructors for the Cavalry and Royal Artillery. This then became the centre from which military show jumping teams were chosen, and where short periods of show jumping training were carried out before a team of officers left for a foreign horse show.

Successive British governments, unlike their European counterparts, took no interest in show jumping; it was more or less left to the private enterprise of instructors at the school, and other interested regimental officers, to devise and practise methods for dealing with their more fortunate European rivals. Progress was therefore bound to be slow, particularly as teams were very seldom sent to Europe, and foreign experience was limited to Dublin and, on two occasions, North America and the big French show at Nice. In addition to this the sport was popular among only a very small minority of officers, and indeed was looked down on by their superiors. Consequently the methods employed were advanced adaptations of the normal jumping instruction for students, and amounted to slow precision riding with its keynote accuracy, based on careful field dressage preparation. The drawback to this method was that successful results were too dependent upon the rider, and uniformity at top level could come about only by chance. But the basic principles were sound and practical, and during the 'thirties were broadened to incorporate considerations such as speed and width of fence construction. Meanwhile, during the 'twenties and 'thirties, great steps had been taken in the presentation of competitions, in the design and construction of courses, and thus in the art of riding over them. The Caprilli followers rightly continued on the lines laid down in his teaching, making adjustments here and there as the situation demanded, the most significant being that as the size of the fences grew it came to be realised that the rider must take some active part in measuring the stride up to the fence. And the growth in size was considerable. The largest fence at the Olympic Games at Stockholm in 1912 measured 4 ft. 6 in. At Berlin in 1936 several stood at 5 ft. 4 in., and difficulties incorporated in the course layout were comparable to those met with in the 'fifties. Fortunately for the post-war future of British show jumping, a small contingent of enthusiastic British civilians, realising in 1922 that there might well be a future for the sport, founded the British Show Jumping Association with the object of standardising the rules, improving courses and encouraging show executives to hold jumping competitions. Although before 1939 this Association was not vested with any great power or authority, and had no hand in international affairs, it was the focal point of British national show jumping. Thus, after the war, and with the disappearance of the horse from the Army, all those interested in show jumping in this country turned to it for help and guidance in the difficult task of re-establishing the sport.

CHAPTER THREE

Post-war Show Jumping 1945–63

At the end of the war show jumping enthusiasts began to put their houses in order, and a great number of the big pre-war national and international shows were revived. But the general set-up, the tempo, and the flavour of the sport at once revealed a change and a sense of forward urgency. Complete mechanisation had sounded the death knell to all but a few of the old Military Cavalry Schools, and international jumping therefore ceased to be a military closed shop. The labours and stresses of war had left a general desire for relaxation, which many people of all types found that riding could provide. As their prowess increased, so their thoughts began to run on competitive lines, and show jumping gave the immediate and most practical answer. The number of competitors advanced by leaps and bounds, and their appetite for learning was a natural corollary. According to the law of averages some were not very good, others were good, and a few were very good indeed. The names of the few began to be known to the general public, who found show jumping an easy and exhilarating sport to watch. Once a name is known it is followed, and interest increases. And with the coming of television not only could the performances of the names be followed through the Press and by hearsay, but they could also be seen. Show jumping at once became a sport that reached every home, and its popularity spread among viewers in all walks of life.

But all sports must have an international flavour to hold permanent public attention and, since the war, jumping has provided this. Every year national teams take part in international competitions, culminating every fourth year in the equestrian events of the Olympic Games. Since 1945 gold medals for show jumping at the Games have attracted nearly every nation. The fortunes of a national jumping team and its components became news, top class jumping gradually developed into a spectator sport, and the skills and techniques required for this class progressed accordingly. The upsurge of public interest and the acceptance of show jumping as a type of competitive sport attainable by so many riders have had far-reaching effects upon its presentation, and encouraged and made necessary progressive advancement in technique. After all, show jumping amounts to a public examination, on competitive lines, of a horse's ability to negotiate cleanly a varied assortment of differently constructed and coloured obstacles, sited at different distances and angles to each other, and of the rider's qualities as a horseman, not only in relation to his competence on the occasion, but also to his proficiency in the preparation for it. To hold public attention by constantly striving to raise the standard, the organisers of the sport worked on the training of horse and rider, setting problems on points of technique by new ideas in the design of courses and in fence construction. There is not a great deal that can be done to alter the structure of obstacles, but the material with which they are built and the solidity of their appearance can greatly influence the horse's and the rider's general attitude to jumping. The horse will be impressed by such fences, will respect them and, provided that he is courageous, he will make a real effort to deal with them effectively. The rider will know that his partner can see the jump, and can make a good estimate of its height and width. He will feel that he has got something to ride at, something to be confident about.

Once this condition has been produced, his confidence will be reflected in the horse by the manner and feel of his riding. Where two very good exponents of the game have that type of communication between them the result can be brilliant. During the 'fifties great strides were made to this end. The circumference of the majority of poles used became greater, the depth of the flat timber used for things such as hurdles or planks grew in size, the elements of completely solid-looking fences such as walls increased in measurement and in weight, the frontage of fences was enlarged, thereby visually reducing the height, and the fittings upon which the elements of a fence rest were given more depth, thus allowing for a reasonable tap, but penalising a mistake. All these factors helped towards free, confident, and bold jumping. By so doing they afforded opportunities for examining the horse's and rider's judgement and effectiveness in the all-important matter of approach, and, not least, they gave the spectators something to look at and talk about, often leading them to suppose that the horses were being asked to overcome greater difficulties than in fact existed. But of greater significance was the increased use of distance and directional problems incorporated in course design. All this aims directly at the standard of the horse's schooling on the flat, and at the rider's judgement, quickness of decision and capabilities of super-accurate control. Fences placed at long distances from each other can be treated as separate entities, and allow the rider time to consider what action by him, if any, is needed in the latter part of the approach to a jump at some distance after landing from the previous one. But when obstacles are sited at a distance of 80 ft. and less from each other he must make his decision as he lands, or before, and the result of his decision will be entirely dependent upon his own and his horse's education in movements on the flat. As I shall explain later, different permutations of distances between different structural types of fences call for different attributes of training. By deduction therefore, various cardinal points of training can be pinpointed for special consideration and attention, so that a new and current problem can be successfully solved. But there can be no question of standing still on acquired knowledge.

Olympic Games awareness, and general acceptance of a gold medal at the Games as the primary aspiration of all show jumpers, has seen to that. With the most prized award to be won each fourth year, competitors are kept permanently on their toes, not only to keep pace with changing conditions, but also to ensure that they and their horses are up to date and entirely familiar with every forecast of new examination problems that may face them on the big day. And new problems are without doubt devised. It is the host nation's duty to design and build the course for the Games, which is kept on the top secret list until competitors are allowed to walk it just before the competition begins. The object of the exercise is to provide a supreme test which is the culmination of four years' preparation. Great difficulties can therefore be expected, but they should be fair and within the physical capabilities of very good and well trained horses. For this reason technical delegates from neutral nations are nominated. These delegates have a preview of the proposed course and fences, and the right to make alterations if necessary. Each successive host nation naturally wishes to make some type of innovation to the course, with the hope that its particular innovation may go down in history as a memorable one.

Any innovation, however slight, calls for some adjustment of riding and training technique, and the result is a constant striving on the one side to present new problems and on the other to surmount them. So the cycle may continue, with the recurring danger that the planners may move right up to, and eventually beyond, the point where a very good horse's physique reaches its limit. This may sound dramatic and somewhat far-fetched, but it is quite possible that a dangerous situation might arise. Such a situation appeared likely to become reality in the 'fifties as many well informed riders and jumping officials expected to see jumps sited at unfair and, except to a very few horses, impracticable distances. Fortunately reason prevailed. Yet who can state positively that a horse's physical limit is a static one, or whether or not it may be stretched a little through some human means? Athletes continue to break world records, presumably with the help of new scientific methods of training that improve their physique and increase their stamina and the effort they can make. Why then should this not be equally applicable to a horse?

There is no doubt that horses are now negotiating greater heights and wider spreads than in pre-war days, but I am by no means convinced that the modern animal is any better equipped physically than his forbears. Nevertheless a similarity in the improved performances of humans and horses can be observed in the rider's assimilation of his capability of playing on the horse's resilience, which is governed by his co-ordination of smooth muscular and mental effort. This can be said to be based on obedience. When obedience is developed to an automatic response to shades of degrees of pace and stride control, newly thought up distances and directional problems can be tackled with confidence.

It is sometimes maintained that distance problems based on mathematical calculations are artificial and, in consequence, breed artificial riding. I do not agree with this opinion. In my view they have two distinct and important commendations. In the first place these calculations obviate the necessity of finding a winner by building fences of great size and, in the second, they cultivate positive and accurate horsemanship and put the horse's education on the flat in the category of match winner. The word positive in this context does entail domination, but the matter of degree enters into it, as refinement of technique cancels any question of force. It is obvious that top class modern international show jumping calls for a very high level of skill and training. Such skill is by no means easily acquired, but the viewing public know it when they see it. Audiences are not prepared to watch mediocrity.

The British Show Jumping Association, finding itself firmly at the helm, was quick to realise that a national sport must have international commitments to hold public interest and to keep pace with progress. But its efforts to achieve them were for a time greatly hampered by the backbone of the Association—the riders and owners, whose attitude remained singularly insular. In addition it took time to bring the fences and courses into a semblance of line with their European counterparts. The chief obstacle in the education of young riders and horses for international jumping was, until 1962, the failure to adopt time as a deciding factor in the rules. The worst result of this was that to attempt to arrive at a definite conclusion course builders were forced to build fences of astronomical dimensions and thus novice horses arriving at Grade A standard were at once grossly over-faced, so that the great majority faded quickly into obscurity, and only a very few outstanding animals went on to the top. This is not simply grumbling for the sake of grumbling. Statistically there has been an alarming drop in the figures of registered horses in the top two grades since the reintroduction in 1958 of Grade B, for horses that have won between £100 and £200. In 1958 there were 493 top, or Grade A, horses, 722 Grade B, and 1,800 Grade C. In 1962 the figures were 347 A, 189 B, and 2,603 C. What then has happened to the 533 in Grade B in 1958 that have disappeared? There is always a certain wastage of figures at the top, and in the middle category; old horses are retired, lameness takes its toll, and there are sales abroad. But the drop is staggering, and I am certain that the main reason has been the size of obstacles, brought about in the first place by the absence of time as a deciding factor, and in the second by the modern highly sponsored open events. I do not wish in any way to decry sponsorship. It has its great and obvious advantages, but big prize money tends to lead to big and

difficult courses, and quite naturally sponsors expect their event
to be the highlight of the programme. The introduction in 1962
of time should gradually right the first of these ills, but the second
needs careful consideration. This is equally applicable to budding
young riders, for too early in life, and with insufficient experience,
they have been plunged into the maelstrom of national open
jumping over fences beyond their scope.

Another post-war national custom, that of the stilted approach
and acrobatic attitude over the fence, did not help. For some
years it was prevalent, mainly from example, but it gradually
became apparent to the young that it was entirely unsuitable not
only for international jumping, but also for the changing national
courses; and by now this unattractive method of riding has, to all
intents and purposes, died an unlamented death. One hindrance
to the preparation for international jumping has yet to be overcome. This is the fact that distance problems, other than those
within double or treble fences, have not been generally considered. Consequently the old habit of treating each fence as
a separate entity, whereby the rider stops proceedings after
jumping one fence and begins to plan anew for the next, is still
in evidence, and is a difficult habit to eradicate. Nevertheless
British performances in the post-war era, although having their
quite understandable ups and downs, have also had their moments
of glory. The Team's gold medal at Helsinki in 1952 was a great
victory, and their bronze at Stockholm in 1956 a very good performance. Their failure in Rome in 1960 was partly compensated
for by a bronze in the individual, while from 1950 to the present
day they have had reasonable success in Nations Cups. The
position at the moment is one that arouses quiet optimism, for
several young riders and horses have come to the front at the
right time before the next Olympics, and should, all going well,
be at their peak by October, 1964. On the whole there is progress,
and the most gratifying point is the growing realisation that
orthodox positions and actions have been designed for purposes
of efficiency, and not solely for the benefit of photographers.

More can be learnt about riding by observation and example
than by reading numerous books on the subject. Obviously the
ideal is to do both, taking care that the first is orthodox to the
extent that the action follows a recognised logical pattern, and
that the second is clear and understandable so that its teachings

take effect when put into practice. A great deal of useful show
jumping information can be gleaned by watching closely the top
riders from foreign countries. At the present time, the most suitable subjects for study are the experienced members of the
American team. They are quiet, effective, and dominant, but
their refinement of controlling technique smothers the use of
force; they are elegant and pleasant to watch and are impeccably
turned out. German theories have influenced their riding, yet
they could not be mistaken for Germans when jumping a round.
Their controlling actions are less evident than those of other
international riders, which speaks highly for their horses' schooling and their technique as riders; their sense of rhythm and their
fluency make for a happy state of confidence. The Germans
themselves are not pretty horsemen, but their systematic effectiveness is beyond question. Team gold medals in 1956 and 1960,
and an individual one in 1956, speak for themselves. Had it not
been for one trick distance in the Rome individual, another gold
could well have come their way. Their guiding principle is complete domination at all times, and the only Caprilli precept followed by them is their attitude over the fence. They are meticulous
in stride control and point of take-off. But in the last few years
the result has been a tendency towards violent checks, and a
sudden rush at a fence from three or four strides, which are not
only a great strain on a horse's physique—a small human error of
judgement can overtax the horse's courage and capability—but
also can easily produce unnecessary time faults. Whether or not
one likes their forcible methods, whether or not one admires their
style of riding, to put it vulgarly they bring home the bacon, and
they can rightly say that that is what is expected of them.

For years now Italy's team has been just the fabulous d'Inzeo
brothers. Other Italian riders have suffered so much by comparison that they have merely been supporting extras. The d'Inzeos
are followers of Caprilli's methods who have made adjustments
to his system to suit prevailing conditions and courses. They
have always been past masters at the art of forward propulsion,
so that, although in general they control the stride and the
take-off platform, they allow for a margin of error, and can
make suggestions to the horse rather than give him a direct order.
They have been so much the main stars that any small crack
in the perfection of their performance has at once been news in

the equestrian press, for they have been the biggest public draw in world jumping. For the past ten years they have been the only exponents of the art of shortening stride by bending the horse's head slightly towards the leading leg; when at the top of their form, their finesse in controlling technique is an object lesson to all show riders.

The Algerian troubles, following those in Indo-China, hit the French hard. They have not been able to field a team of any merit since 1959. This has been a great loss to the sport. French riding through the centuries has been noted for its gaiety, its beauty and its dash. One hopes that, with the return of stability, a new French team will emerge, no doubt trained in the old tradition of free forward riding. The Spaniards have also faded from the scene. Some of the riders who do appear from Spain seem to be in doubt about what method of riding to adopt. At one moment they release the horse, as much as to say, 'There you are, and now make the best of it yourself', and the next they check him hard, and begin trying to make tentative arrangements themselves. It seems that any form of directive is missing, and that they are moving in the dark. The Irish Free State Military team is comparable, and lacks decisiveness in control and training, while the Iron Curtain countries remain an enigma. Their sorties into the western world since the war have not been impressive, but the Russians seem to work under French influence, and they could well make themselves felt in a few years time. The two leading South American countries, Chile and the Argentine, are both of the Caprilli school, but have followed the leading Italian riders in the method of control during the latter part of the approach, and their riding is accurate, attractive, and fluent.

What then of the world in general? It seems to me that degree of riding ability is taking a perfectly natural course. As difficulties of course design and fence construction increase, so the number of riders who can deal with them decreases. The number of really top line show jumping riders is therefore small, and any nation is fortunate if it can muster three. This does not mean that international jumping is declining. With the exception of some of the small countries that have not yet recovered from the war, and which before it relied on their cavalry, and of the Iron Curtain countries which, as vassal states, are allowed no initiative, there are numerous riders who fill the second and third line positions and are the real backbone of the sport. So it is the few that the public want to see, and it is the many who make the whole sport possible. This may seem unfair, particularly when the few are also more likely to benefit from the big sponsored competitions, but without perpetual search for perfection there can be no hope of progress. This post-war period does leave one anachronism in show jumping which could be righted with one simple reform. It is high time that show jumping riders became known as riders, without the outmoded and much abused label of amateur or professional.

4. *The approach. Myself, riding 'Red Port'.*

5. *The take-off. Miss Mary Mairs, U.S.A., riding 'Tomboy' at the White City.*

6. The airborne period. Miss Anneli Drummond-Hay on 'Merely-a-Monarch' at Hickstead.

CHAPTER FOUR

Present-day Requirements for Horse and Rider

What then are the chief requirements for horse and rider to stand a reasonable chance of attaining fame in the show jumping world? The ideal must always be aimed at, and an analysis of each case will help to paint a realistic picture of essential fundamentals, in what one hopes to find, in what one hopes to be, and in what one hopes to produce. Finding the right horse is probably the most difficult problem. There never has been, and no doubt never will be, a pattern of horseflesh that always makes a good jumper. In fact the reverse is true. Often the most unlikely looking animals lead the field, while a horse appearing to have all the necessary qualifications turns out to be a dismal failure. I think that this is one of the main attractions in the search for novice jumpers. A horse bought for a song—preferably one spurned by everyone else—that turns up trumps must inevitably give boundless satisfaction. Nevertheless a prospective buyer should have some sort of picture in his mind of what he is looking for. There are various points of conformation which should logically be important, not only to ensure power, liberty and durability, but also to enable the animal to undergo the intensive schooling necessary.

The power of propulsion which enables a horse to jump great heights and spreads comes from behind—a short back, strong quarters, a wide, well rounded loin to allow muscle development, plenty of length from hip to hock, robust second thighs, not too straight a hind leg, the hocks large and low; all these will help to produce it; while a tail well set on, and nice and high, is a sign of strength. A suitable horse should have good depth of girth, and therefore heartroom, and should 'follow' well. In other words, his ribs should be rounded and well sprung, so that when standing behind him one can see the 'fullness' of the ribs outside the quarters. These good points will conserve the power and give stamina. But power alone is not enough. The present-day jumper must have liberty, and the shoulder, neck and withers will have a great deal to do with this. The withers should be well developed, running into the back and just higher than the quarters. The shoulder needs to be sloping, with length from its point to the withers, while the neck should slip into the shoulder, be strong, moderately long, and nicely arched. Great store should be set on the type of neck, as it will affect action and carriage. Another important factor is the chest, as it contains the breathing organs. A deep broad one will give room for the organs to function properly, encouraging freedom and stamina, and will carry the girth well. The slope and length of the pastern bone is applicable here; a short upright one can make the action stumpy and lessen natural spring, and if very long and sloping, the horse will not stand up to hard work. No jumper can be of permanent value unless he has durability and can work hard for long periods on all types of going. Despite these remarks on the pastern bone, it is the feet that count most. They need to be open, nicely rounded, with ample room for a clean elastic frog, and equal in shape and size. Above them the fetlock joints should be flat and pronounced, the cannon bones short and strong, the knee low down, large and flat, and the forearm long with width for the development of strong muscles. The whole foreleg to the fetlock joint should be straight, with no suspicion of being back at the knee.

Finally comes the head. Many people will buy a horse if they like his head, despite other failings, and will reject him if the head is not to their taste. There is a great deal in this. After all, the head houses the brain and controls the animal's mental make-up. Bad temper and cowardice must be avoided at all costs. Choose, therefore, a head of medium dimensions with the forehead broad between the eyes. Let the line from the forehead to the nose be straight, and be certain that there is ample room between the jaw bone and the throat. The eyes should be full and have a wide range of vision, giving the horse a good expression, and the ears should be well pricked and not too large. Such an animal is easy to write about, but the dickens of a job to find.

Breeding must also be considered. Attempts have been made

for years to breed show jumpers with no apparent success although there is no doubt that the progeny of certain sires will always leave the ground well, and many a mother passes on her natural spring. Nevertheless, whatever the breeding, the animal must have quality. Logically, a thorough bred animal should be the type required. With time the deciding factor in all competitions except the puissance and nations cups, a horse needs an easy turn of foot so that he can always be moving well within himself. But clean bred horses take a long time to train, as they tend to be excitable and over-keen, and the great majority, oddly enough, are lacking in courage at critical moments. However, the common type of animal will very seldom have the pace or resilience to cope with modern conditions and distances, so that a well-made, good dispositioned three-quarter bred horse, combining substance and quality, and standing about 16.2 hands high, will in the end be the best bet. Such animals are now, alas, rare. Mechanisation in Irish farming has made the Irish light draught mare redundant, but although this has seriously curtailed the output such animals still appear on the market. If one is fortunate in finding one, and it has the other necessary attributes, there is no reason why it should not be trained into the top class.

Whatever problems there may be facing a horse used for show jumping, virtues in his conformation seem illogically to be the least important. The main ones can be divided into two categories, physical and mental. Physically he must have a natural spring, enabling him to jump great heights and spreads easily. If the spring is a supple one, produced by his making use of his back, loins, head and neck, and if he naturally folds his legs well up, he will start with a great advantage. With conformation lending a helping hand, different parts of his anatomy must be capable of undergoing the stresses and strains of intensive training, and the quality of his general physique should enable him to be schooled to deal with distance problems on the flat. His mental set-up is of the highest importance. He must obviously like jumping, and dislike making mistakes. He must be very bold and courageous. A bold horse will take any obstacle in his path, and a really courageous one will continue to give of his best through thick and thin, and in all kinds of conditions. It is comparatively easy to pick out boldness, but courage can be determined only in adversity. It will help if he has the natural ability to extricate himself from awkward situations, and if he has a well-developed sense of his own stride arrangements when jumping loose. A calm disposition will foster reliability and make the training easier, but great keenness must be there, with the nerves taut, but controlled. A really great horse will sense the big occasion and rise to it. All this will call for intelligence and sensitivity above the average, although some extremely intelligent animals decide very definitely quite early in their careers that they like fox-hunting very much indeed, but that show jumping is a very poor form of sport! Then comes the question, is it better to look for a big horse or a little one? A 'good big 'un' is said to have the beating of a 'good little 'un'. But a big horse with quality and substance is not easy to find. Furthermore, his training presents greater difficulty than usually occurs with a smaller horse and is mainly associated with balance, the heart of all jumping. On the other hand, a big horse with the main requirements to his credit will deal easily with big fences and long distances that would stretch a small one to the limit. His activity cannot be so elastic, and his durability is less likely to be so lasting. There are the normal exceptions to either choice, and the general opinion tends towards a horse of medium size, one combining power with activity, reliability with brilliance, and one that can be schooled and trained in a reasonably short time.

Good show jumping is a partnership, and however excellent the horse may be, only reasonable results can be expected when the rider is just adequate. Real and consistent success can be achieved only when the rider is an expert who not only has the knowledge, but also the ability to put that knowledge into practice. Now that show jumping courses have become so severe, the top class rider needs to be an artist in that particular kind of jumping. He should be a show jumping *horseman*, a man who has gone beyond being merely a show jumping *rider*, as this type of jumping is now a spectator sport. However expert he may be technically he should have other attributes if he wants to reach the top and stay there. A natural flair is a very pleasant thing to have; it is found now and then in all sports, and show jumping is no exception. Dedication and singleness of purpose are necessities for any great sport, and considerable powers of concentration can develop them. The will to win against any odds can often tip the scales, and some people have a remarkable gift of rising to the big occasion. Confidence in one's ability will communicate

7. *The landing. Captain A. Queipo de Llano, Spain, riding 'Eolo IV'*
at the White City.

8. *The get-away after landing. Peter Robeson riding 'Firecrest' at the*
White City.

9. *An upright fence at Rotterdam.*

10. *A parallel fence at Ostend.*

itself to the horse, and thus form the bedrock of a real partnership, and a quick, sensitive, and intuitive brain will make split-second decisions so that any tricky situation is never out of hand, and unforeseen difficulties are anticipated. Steady nerve and quiet courage will make for consistency in the face of adversity and when the time comes, all the stops can be pulled out with the sole object of winning.

The acquired skills that must be part and parcel of the show jumping rider's equipment can then be formulated, backed by his mental ability. Riders can be divided into three categories. There are those who ride for fresh air and exercise, to escape from their anxieties; the rudiments of steerage and staying on the animal are sufficient for them. Secondly there are those who want to know more about riding, technically, and want to become sufficiently good horsemen to be able to enjoy a sport involving riding, such as fox-hunting. Finally there are the horsemen who specialise in one particular branch of competitive or exhibition riding—'haute école', combined training, flat racing, steeple-chasing, or show jumping. The moment a job becomes special-ised, accuracy is the keynote to success. In show jumping, where a human being and an animal must work in harmony and under-standing, accuracy must be maintained not only in the concep-tion of what is to be aimed at, but also in every detailed thought and action leading to the ultimate goal. The horseman should have in his mind a clear picture of what he and his horse should look like, and of how each separate movement should be carried out, so that his performance not only brings its reward, but also provides an impressive and pleasing spectacle to the paying public, to whom the show jumper has a very definite obligation. It is not always appreciated, I think, that during his time in the arena the horseman is in a somewhat similar position to that of an actor. He should provide value for money, otherwise attendance figures will dwindle and a situation could develop when, for economic reasons, show organisers would no longer be willing to stage show jumping events. It is therefore in his own interests, and for the benefit of the sport in general, that his style, efficiency, and beha-viour warrant public approval. I cannot stress too much that specialisation demands accuracy, and accuracy must come from a comprehensive knowledge of a logical and reasoned method of schooling and training a suitable horse, and of an equally logical

and reasoned method of riding him. This knowledge embraces a
wealth of detailed information which must be sorted out into
basic factors. Once these have been determined, hours of con-
centrated and patient practice are necessary, so that ultimately
the partnership between man and horse leads to the required
result.

It is necessary for the show jumping horseman to decide definitely the overall method he intends to use. Is he going to take
complete control, which will automatically entail dominating the
stride during the approach to each fence, and determining the
platform from which the horse takes off, or is he going to leave
these two problems for the horse to solve? In support of the latter
method it can be said that a good horse jumping loose will seldom
make a mistake, so why not hand the problem over to him entirely? At the beginning of the century, obstacles were small and
simple, and this method, as advocated by Caprilli, worked perfectly well. But—and a very big but it is—times have changed
radically. The tremendous increase in size, the more complicated
construction of fences and, recently, the introduction of examination by distance, have raised the issue so much that it is neither
reasonable nor possible for the horse to bear full responsibility.
The consensus of enlightened opinion has for some time been
that full control is essential for success at the top level. Control
and quiet happy dominance will produce the best results without any shadow of doubt.

The modern show jumping horseman must learn to ride with
precision at a speed to suit the conditions of the event. The
result will be the sum total accruing from the information mentioned above, and the overall picture of horse and rider will be
one of rhythmical and fluent accuracy of movement on the flat,
and during the jump itself; so the basic factors upon which the
horseman must rely for his acquired skills hinge on rhythm,
fluency, and accuracy, the co-ordination of the three producing
the required precision. It will help to clarify the position if the
complete result, or the whole show jumping round, is divided into
clear-cut and separate phases. To the spectator, and in the horse's
estimation, the round should flow as one entity and as one operation. If then the rider can develop accuracy in each phase, he
will be in a position to mould them into one fluent and rhythmic
movement; I suggest that a round logically divides itself into five

separate parts. The approach (Plate 4) consists of all the time spent on the flat from before passing through the start until just after passing through the finish, thus entailing changes of direction. The take-off (Plate 5) occupies a very short time, from when the first of the horse's fore feet leave the ground until the last of the hind follow suit. While the height and width of the fence are being cleared the horse is airborne (Plate 6), and this is closely followed by the landing (Plate 7), when first the fore and then the hind feet regain terra firma. Lastly comes the get-away-after-landing, comprising the first two or three strides on the flat which are, in effect, the beginning of the next part of the approach (Plate 8). Each of these phases needs careful study. An understanding of the mechanics of the horse's movement on the flat, and when jumping, will help to evolve methods of producing accuracy without loss of freedom and natural liberty, and to determine for the rider the best position for him to adopt on the horse, so that he can synchronise his own movements and, at the same time, give the necessary indications for complete control.

A show jumper must be a trained horse, one that responds to his rider's intention from his least movement rightly, lightly, and with energy. To act rightly he must be instantaneously obedient to the lightest indication. To be light he must be in a suitable state of balance for the demands of the immediate occasion. To supply energy he must first of all be performing rightly and lightly, so that all his forces of energy can be gathered together and held by the rider to form impulsion, which can then be exploited by him as and when he sees fit. And before any of these qualities can materialise to the highest degree, the horse must be perfectly acquainted with free forward movement, or acceleration and deceleration. Now, although the acquisition of these basic attributes will be helped by sensitivity, temperament, conformation, and a spirit of willing co-operation, they cannot approach perfection without expert and reasoned actions on the part of the rider. So it is for the show jumping horseman to develop his skill with these four basic factors in view. A firm and independent type of position on the horse's back will not only ensure harmony and correct weight distribution for the furtherance of the balance of the whole mass, but will also make it possible for the rider to employ each part of his own anatomy to give clear signals of his intentions. Thus a stable and uniform position, coupled with clear and sympathetic indications, will produce a firm bond of confidence between the two partners, resulting in precision at the pace required. The acquired skills necessary for any type of specialised job are far-reaching. For show jumping I shall always maintain that a riding background that has involved the difficult as well as the rosy paths, one that has had its ups and downs and rough going, will be advantageous in the long run. In this country fox-hunting provides it.

CHAPTER FIVE

Some Technical Problems Set for Horse and Rider

Before dealing with the ways and means of developing the rider's skill, and of educating the horse to the desired pitch, it will be as well to have a clear understanding of the problems to be faced. As previously mentioned, they will be presented in the form of an examination of the horse's jumping ability and standard of training, and of the quality of the rider's general horsemanship. This will take concrete shape in the type and construction of fences, in course design, and in the siting of the obstacles along the route. A careful study of the current trend in these matters will indicate the lines along which training should be carried out and, if innovations are spotted, deductions can be made to adjust schooling methods to deal effectively with them.

Structurally there are only four types of fence: the upright (Plate 9), parallel (Plate 10), staircase (Plate 11), and pyramid (Plate 12). The variation of types governs the distance from the first element of the fence to the take-off point, or platform, from which it is most suitable for the horse to jump cleanly, and without the expenditure of unnecessary effort, while the structure of each type affects the angle of descent to the landing, which, in turn, affects the first and second strides taken by the horse after landing. An appearance of solidity or flimsiness, and sharply contrasting colours, present their own separate problems. A true upright fence is one whose elements are in the same vertical plane, the extreme instances being a single pole or plank, and a straight-faced wall. If augmented by a thick solid ground line, placed in front and away from it, the jump ceases to be an upright, and is only related to it on a cousinly basis. A true parallel type is one in which the two top elements are separated to form a

41

spread and are of the same height. Here the extremes are two
single poles at a distance of, say, 4 ft. from each other, and two
walls similarly sited. This sort of obstacle provides great scope for
variation and imaginative building, and its degree of difficulty
can be altered to suit different occasions; for instance, if the two
top elements are not of identical height, and if a forward ground
line is added, the problem is simplified. The staircase has three
distinct parts, the top element of each gaining height away from
the take-off side. Again this can be bare, consisting only of three
poles, or it can be filled in with three hedges or walls, each with a
pole over it. It also lends itself to different patterns: the staircase
can be steep or flat, convex or concave; the centre stair can be
omitted, transforming it into an open ditch without the ditch.
It can therefore be quite a simple affair, or very difficult indeed.
The pyramid is also a three-dimensional structure, with the
greatest height in the centre. In its simplest form, three poles with
filling under the first two, it is the easiest of show fences. But its
offshoots can be far from straightforward. A solid, wide, rounded
affair, shaped like a roll-top desk or field pigsty (Figure 1), is
very impressive, and produces a steep descent to landing; and a
water jump, with fence in front, is like a pyramid less the last two
elements. A horse should jump it in the same style as for a normal
pyramid. With plenty of good material, and with the help of
a lively imagination, all these types of fence can have variations

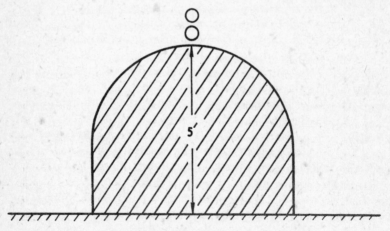

Fig. 1. A roll-top desk or field pigsty type of fence

which help to make the course attractive, and which provide different degrees of test to suit different grades of competition.

Various facts then clearly emerge. The platform from which a horse can most suitably take-off varies in distance from the fence according to its type, shape, and size. An upright allows for the greatest margin of error. Up to a height of 4 ft. 8 in., a similar distance away can be taken as a useful guide to the convenient point. But a horse blessed with great liberty can manage a far wider distance, and an athletic one can come in close. A staircase has the opposite effect. Owing to the fact that the point of maximum height coincides with the far limit of the width, the ideal take-off platform is obviously close to the first stair, or element, of the jump. A parallel can have equal height at both limits of the width, and so, to make the first height and the extent of the spread, the take-off must move back, and be decided by the measurements of the fence. This calls for great accuracy. The far element of an orthodox pyramid is of little consequence, in that if the centre one is cleared freely the horse's line of flight will carry him over it. Such a jump is therefore simply a distant cousin to an upright, or a staircase with only two stairs. There is then, up to a height of 4 ft. 8 in., a wide margin of error, governed to an extent by the natural length of the horse's stride. It will, however, be wise to deal with it as a two-stair staircase, and come in close.

Pyramid offshoots are more complex. The pigsty type has an extensive and solid base and middle width, and should be treated as a parallel. A water jump, with or without a pole over it, makes a wide spread, and the take-off platform must therefore be very close to the element immediately in front of the water itself. A heavily built and solid obstacle is impressive. It gives horse and rider something to look at and so encourages bold and free action, but a flimsy construction generates caution. Distinctive and startling colours call for a bold outlook, and can hold attention to the exclusion of other important things. The shape and size of a fence govern the parabola of the horse's jump, which itself determines the angle of descent to the landing point. If this angle is shallow, the horse can move off into his normal stride immediately after landing. But, if the angle of descent is steep, he will tend to pitch, thus cramping his natural movement. Fences causing a steep descent are those of a high, wide variety, those with an impressively solid, wide base, carrying smaller

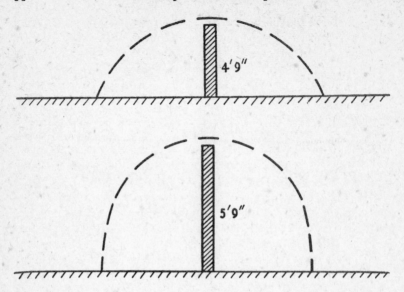

*Fig. 2. The angle of descent becomes steeper as the height increases
above 4 ft. 9 in.*

elements above, and any fence having a height of 4 ft. 9 in., or
more (Figure 2).

These conditions present their particular problems, but deduction can find a solution to each. The rider will need to start by
ensuring that the horse has every reasonable chance of jumping
each fence cleanly. To effect this he must complete each part of
the approach on the suitable take-off platform. This entails
meticulous control of the stride by the rider, assisted by the
horse's own eye and natural judgement. But to reach the ultimate end—precision at the required speed—control must be
equally certain at any pace. This at once introduces basic factors
in training, split second free forward movement, implicit obedience to hand and leg indications and, above all, a state of
fluid balance by which the centre of gravity of the mass of the
horse's and rider's weights is such as to allow free forward movement and obedience to reach a degree of perfection. This enables
the rider to make adjustments to the overall length of the horse's
stride during the latter part of each part of the approach, with

11. *A staircase fence. Miss Ann Townsend winning the Puissance at Madrid in 1959 on 'Bandit'. The fence stood at 6' 7" in height, with a spread of 7' 6". (Photograph: L'Année Hippique, Lausanne)*

12. *A pyramid fence.*

13. *Collection at the canter. Mrs V. D. S. Williams on 'Little Model'.*

14. *The shoulder-in, showing clearly the separate tracks taken by the fore and hind legs. Mrs V. D. S. Williams on 'Little Model'.*

the result that the fall of the horse's fore feet, followed by the hind, coincide with the desired take-off platform. Fluency is vital without any sharp contrast of pace. For the operation to be successful the rider must be placed on the horse's back so that he is at all times in balance with the rhythm of the horse's movement, and in a position to employ the controlling parts of his own anatomy independently of each other, thus imparting to the horse precise and clear-cut instructions.

Solid looking fences call for a horse with a bold, keen, and freedom-loving temperament, while flimsies require a lighter shade of obedience, the certainty that the parabola of the jump is of the right shape, and that the fore and hind legs are well folded. The first is in Nature's hands, but the second can be taught. One luridly coloured jump in a course can breed suspicion in the boldest of horses and can upset his concentration. Sensible schooling will minimise such failings. Many a steeplechase has been lost through a horse dwelling on landing, and the fault applies equally to show jumping. When a fence is of a shape or size that dictates a steep angle of descent to the ground, momentum is dissipated and the horse, through pitching, cannot stretch forward the normal distance for the first stride after landing. Not only is pace decreased, but rhythm also alters, and a new operation has to be begun. When distance problems are involved the battle is lost before the next jump is within striking distance. The answer is, of course, in the other basic factor, impulsion, or the harnessing of the horse's forces of energy by the rider, so that extra effort can be called on at will. In this case the release of some of the impulsion held will keep the pace and stride the same as before take-off.

The course design is the plan of the route to be taken in the arena. The majority of arenas in the world are of uniform shape— square, rectangular, round or oval. Those at Aachen and Rotterdam are notable exceptions, the former being very large with two non-parallel sides, one curved end, and the other as two sides of a flat triangle; the latter has sides and ends which are not parallel, so that one corner is almost a peninsula. Some, such as Wiesbaden, Lucerne, and Rotterdam, contain live trees and shrubs, and many have permanent and growing jumps; Lucerne and Aachen, among others, have a widely assorted variety. Such grounds are used only for horse shows. The shape and size

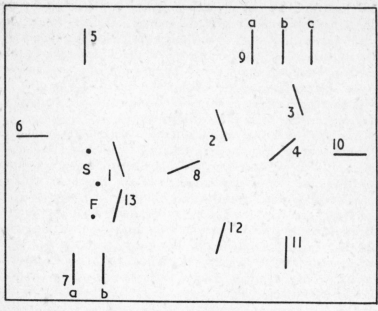

Fig. 3. A difficult course, designed from a figure-of-8 base

directly affect possible and reasonable routes, but more often than not a design is based on a figure-of-8 (Figure 3), a general lay-out that can be fitted into an arena of any dimensions. Whatever the shape of the route, the relevant fact is the matter of changing direction. It must be taken for granted that those responsible for the building of courses, and those undertaking the thankless task of judging, agree with competitors that a show jumping round must be ridden as one operation, and not as separate bits and pieces with a shuddering check between each. Although therefore changes of direction can be expected to be acute, it should still be feasible to maintain a reasonably uniform pace. For an ordinary competition the route may demand four or five changes of rein, but in speed events many more may be planned, making the whole route extremely circuitous. The rider and the horse must learn to carry out changes of direction of any angle at different speeds, and they must both be able to follow exactly the track on the ground predetermined by the rider during his inspection of the course on foot. Following the track exactly cannot be achieved unless the changes of direction are accurate. Problems of design are logically solved when the horse is trained to the extent of moving in a high state of fluid balance, of changing direction with suppleness of neck and back, and bending towards the direction of movement, so that at all times his hind feet follow in the track of the fore.

Let us now consider the siting of the fences along the route. The way in which they are placed in relation to each other, and to changes of direction, forms the basis of the examination of a trained horse and an experienced rider. Siting problems can be threefold. Consecutive fences can be of different structural types, calling for a variation of pace and of position for take-off. Balance must change in relation to pace. Fences may be placed a few strides after the completion of a change of direction, making the straight part of that segment of the approach short—this usually happens coming away from the end of the arena—and in this instance accuracy in following the planned track is essential, so that full use can be made of available ground space. Maintenance of impulsion throughout the change of direction itself will ensure sufficient momentum for the horse to jump freely and naturally, whatever the type of fence. Jumps can be built at distances which do not always coincide with the length of an even number of strides taken by a normal horse. In fact distance problems can be introduced. Fences can be sited in relation to each other in three different ways. They may be entirely unrelated, they may be related, or they may be closely related in the form of doubles or trebles, when more than one jump constitutes a single fence.

The status of relationship or non-relationship is determined by the distance between them, measured from the element on the landing side of the first, to the element on the take-off side of the next, or inside to inside. At more than 80 ft. apart jumps can be dealt with separately, and are unrelated. Between 80 ft. and 39 ft. 4 in. they are related, as the jumping of the second is directly affected by the horse's movements and the rider's actions immediately on landing over the first. Below 39 ft. 4 in. jumps, according to the rules, become part of a combination fence and are closely related, there being only one or two non-jumping strides between them, making the jumping of the second even more dependent upon what happens on landing over the first. The main objective of all course builders should be the encouragement of free, fluent jumping, so in competitions of minor stature, and in events for novice horses and riders, distance problems should not be introduced.

In other words, the distance between closely related jumps and related fences should be such that an even number of a normal horse's strides coincide with the distance between the points of landing and take-off. In competitions for more advanced horses and riders this need not be so. If in a closely related fence the distance is slightly increased, there will be, say, $1\frac{1}{8}$ normal strides instead of 1; if slightly decreased, there will be only, say, $\frac{7}{8}$ of a normal stride. In related fences an increase can make $4\frac{1}{3}$ strides instead of 4, or a decrease $3\frac{2}{3}$ instead of 4. If the distance does not suit a horse's stride, the rider has to devise a method by which he disposes of the fraction of stride over or below the number that does suit. Obviously, if a 1 stride double measures long, the non-jumping one must be lengthened and, if short, it must be shortened. When the number presented is $4\frac{1}{2}$, the rider has the option of making it 4 or 5 (Figure 4). Provided that pace is uniform, there can never be more than $\frac{1}{2}$ a stride to be disposed of, since 3 plus $\frac{3}{4}$ is the same as 4 minus $\frac{1}{4}$. It must be remembered that an uphill gradient, or soft going, in the arena will lengthen the distance, whereas a downhill gradient, or hard going, will shorten it. Such problems can be linked with others based on fence construction. Take two fences, the first a wide and high pigsty type, and the second a parallel, sited at a 4 non-jumping stride interval. The make, shape, size, and impressive appearance of the first will join forces to enforce a steep angle of descent. This will

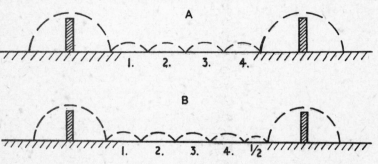

Fig. 4. A. Two fences sited for a normal 4 stride distance. B. Two fences setting a problem by adding half a stride to the distance

15. *Moving*
round a circular
manège at a
balanced canter.

16. 'Red Port' in a state of balance which can be adjusted at will to suit variations of pace.

tend to make the first stride after landing shorter than normal, and thus a distance that measures to suit becomes difficult, owing to the danger of a disposal problem materialising as well. If such a situation occurs in a double or treble fence, the difficulties become accentuated. Many different lessons must therefore be learned by horse and rider before such problems can be treated as routine matters. The rider must be able to calculate, by his own step measurement, whether or not the distances in the course are suitable for the stride of his particular horse. This again emphasises the importance of the time allowed him to inspect the course on foot. From his calculations he must form a plan of campaign to cope with any adjustments necessary in stride control within related or closely related fences. The disposal of unwanted fractions of a stride is synonymous with the necessary adjustments and, when carried out to perfection, bears the hallmark of real artistry. The pace should remain the same, except when the dictates of fence construction call for a transition, and then it must be smooth and fluent. The horse's head carriage should be low and constant, to ensure a convex rounding of the back and a proper engagement of the hind legs. The horse should accept the bit softly, without resentment, from a firm, but sympathetic indication from the rider. The balance must be of top quality, and impulsion produced and maintained, so that the required adjustment is barely perceptible. The animal must be a trained horse, and his human partner must be expert at his specialised job. I have said before that perfection may be just round the corner and one might, one day just reach it. But a perfectionist pure and simple, lacking a streak of ruthlessness and the will to win, may well be a bitter disappointment and, in reverse and quite inadvertently, a practical advertisement for forcible and unattractive methods.

Part Two

THE WAYS AND MEANS

General Considerations

Principles of Training for Movement on the Flat

Development of the Horse's Jumping Skill

The Rider

Jumping the Round

Inspection of the Course on Foot:
Bridles—Martingales—Nose Bands

Conclusion

PART TWO

CHAPTER ONE

General Considerations

Ruskin's remark that 'it is far more difficult to be simple than to be complicated' has often been quoted. This is certainly true of authors on show jumping whose writings are often so intensely involved that beginners must find it hard to separate the wood from the trees. I will therefore set myself a difficult task and endeavour to be simple. In earlier chapters I have tried to indicate what is required of horse and rider, and have outlined some of the problems that must be faced. Next must come a clarification of the two important essentials—a logical and reasoned method of schooling and training a suitable horse, and an equally logical and reasoned method of riding him. Obviously a beginner cannot be expected to school a horse. He must first be trained himself, so that he can act clearly in a teaching capacity. I do not propose to explain the primary steps to be taken in the education of an unbroken horse, nor the instruction necessary for a new recruit to riding. I intend to consider a horse whose natural jumping form and whose mental equilibrium seem to warrant his being tried as a show jumper, and a reasonably talented ordinary horseman who has become interested in competitive jumping.

It has been accepted that to reach the top in modern show jumping the rider must be prepared to take full control. Success in achieving this depends upon three factors; first, the horse's jumping capability and temperament; second, the horse's education in movement on the flat, and development of his jumping skill; and third, the rider's position or attitude on the horse's back at all paces and during the jump. The first of these is incorporated in the requirements for the horse. His temperament can often be influenced by kindliness and tact, and his latent jumping potential can be developed during his training. The second and third are completely interwoven with one another. Nevertheless an inexperienced, but reasonably talented horseman can improve his horse, provided that he understands what he is aiming at, the logical sequence of lessons leading to that end, and the reasons for them.

Before going any further I think it as well to consider the word dressage, and its implications. Dressage is a French word and, in its native sense, means schooling. When first used by the French in a riding context it referred to the preparation for manège riding, leading to the high school. At that time no other form of specialised riding was practised and, from the elementary level, it was based on collection, and on giving the horse a central balance. When, in the present century, competitions for cross-country work and jumping were introduced, the French, who must be expected to be the best judges of the meaning of their own language, realised that the word alone did not accurately describe the preparation for them. It continued to imply only preparation for manège riding. Being sticklers for accurate expression, a clear differentiation was made by calling the old system Dressage de Manège, and the new Dressage Sportif. These definitions were further broken down into Dressage Académique for high school, and Dressage d'Obstacles for work over fences only. This differentiation did not become universal. Most equestrians, certainly in this country, used and continue to use the word dressage by itself, implying that the animal is schooled in a similar fashion on the flat for any type of riding, be it high school, three day event, show jumping, steeplechasing, foxhunting, or simply hacking. The result, in my opinion, is a muddled idea of the particular objective, and the approach to it.

Having asked various riders what they intended to do on their horses for the next hour, I have often been told, 'Oh! a bit of dressage'. I have often wondered what exactly they mean. Do they imply practice at a set manège test? If they simply mean a bit of schooling, for what purpose is it to be done, and what type of schooling anyhow? Do they realise that the word dressage, in its purest sense, has its foundation on collection? If this is so, is it to be understood that a degree of enforced collection is an integral part of the horse's education for any type of riding? It is time the word dressage ceased to be used in a loose sense. In international riding, French is the first language, English the the second. The French understood clearly that it was a fallacy to base preparation for the new types of competitive riding, cross-country and jumping, on enforced collection, and amended their methods and phraseology accordingly. I suggest that English-speaking riders should follow suit; by all means borrow and make use of the word dressage, but for goodness sake let us advance with the times, and give the word additional and descriptive labels as the French have done; divide the general implications of dressage into two main categories, field dressage as the title for the preparation for cross-country and jumping work, and manège dressage for work to be done only on the flat and at slow paces, leading to the high school. I am certain that if such a distinction were to be universally accepted, methods of training for a specific purpose would be clarified, and so gain in simplicity. Then the question of whether or not any degree of collection is needed could be resolved by the particular type of effort and movement required from the horse in the particular department of riding for which he is being prepared. The question of course hinges upon the derivation of the word 'collection'. A 'collected' horse is one whose overall weight distribution, or centre of gravity, is placed to the rear of his centre, and held there for a period of time while the horse is either stationary or at the walk, trot or canter. The energy generated by such a state of balance is brought about by the flexion of the hocks, by the lowering of the croup, by the raising of the neck, and by placing the face on an almost vertical plane. It is obvious that a horse in such a physical state will not be able to handle himself cleverly when given freedom of the head and neck, and will not be capable of adjusting his equilibrium at fast paces (Plate 13).

THE HORSE: HIS NERVOUS SYSTEM

A horse must be trained with kindness, encouragement, firmness when required, and above all with patience. So that the rider can be in clear and direct communication with his horse there has to be a system for passing messages. The system used is based on the association of ideas and sensations, working on the horse's nervous system. This can be divided into three parts—sensory nerves, brain, and motor nerves. Sensory nerves, situated in the mouth, lips, tongue and skin, are to be found all over the horse, and are nerves of feeling. The least pressure or impression on them causes a current to pass to the horse's brain. The endings of these sensory nerves are in the brain, and where they end is considered to be the centre of memory and consciousness, but not, as in the human frame, a centre of reason. Although a horse has a limited intelligence, his brain is characterised by the housing of a marvellous memory, a remarkable power of observation and a lively imagination. The last quality is the cause of fear, and so of the many reactions produced by it. The motor nerves start from the brain and pass down to, and command, the muscles of the body. If an impression or current passes down a motor nerve, the muscle governed by that motor nerve moves. Messages are therefore passed from the rider by his producing a particular sensation or impression on a particular part of the body, which, by continual repetition, and reward and correction, associates a particular movement in the horse's memory. Such sensations and impressions are commonly called the Aids, and are the rider's indications to the horse for purposes of control. To produce complete clarity the sensation associated with a specific movement or reaction must be given at the same place, on the same sensory nerve, every time it is used. Even a slight alteration can confuse the memory, and the consequent reaction will not be either accurate or immediate. At first, impressions will need to be strong and firm but, as the lesson becomes better known to the memory, the time lag between the arrival of the impression in the brain and the required action by the muscle will decrease. Gradually the strength of the impression can be decreased until the final objective is reached and the lightest impression is simultaneous with the required reaction. When accuracy is not all-important, an intelligent horse will respond slowly to straightforward impressions, even if they are somewhat misplaced, but in specialised riding such as show jumping, accuracy is imperative, and this cannot be expected unless the horse's reception of each impression is so clearly understood that the reaction is automatic. Always give your horse the best possible chance. The smooth and efficient working of this communication system forms the foundation of effective and attractive show jumping.

SOME RULES OF TRAINING

Having decided on the methods of communication with his horse, the rider must then embark on his education by following a collection of principles and rules established by experience, and justified by reason. Reasonable rules are usually a matter of common sense. For instance, position should always precede movement. If the trainer is going to ask his horse to perform an exercise which is strange to him, he should first place him in a position from which he may most easily begin it, aided by the laws of nature and movement, and according to his muscular development. This rule can be carried further. If the rider is merely practising his horse in any movement already known to him, he will be well advised to choose a piece of ground which will help to make the particular exercise easy. Again, it must never be forgotten that a tired muscle is a stiff muscle. Stiffness must be avoided at all costs, as sooner or later, at first from weariness and then from pain, the horse will attempt to evade the use of that muscle and thus learn disobedience. It follows that it is necessary for a trainer to be able to differentiate between an evasion and a defence. His decision must affect his reaction and his action. An evasion needs correction until it ceases, while a defence must be attacked and punished in a good-natured manner at once.

An evasion, simply a passing attempt to side-step the issue, can arise from over-freshness, lack of knowledge, a breakdown in the communication system, weariness, or pain. A defence is active resistance. If disregarded, it can become a permanent error. The odd horse can inherit a streak of 'bloody-mindedness', but more often some past unpleasant incident has remained indelibly imprinted on his memory. It must be remembered that a healthy horse should look and feel well. A kick and a squeal are healthy signs—the animal is only giving vent to his feelings. A lesson therefore should never be begun while the horse is suffering from exuberant spirits, or vibrating from the influence of fear or excitement. Steady exercise will be necessary before concentration and full reception can be attained. These, as I said, are all matters of common sense, but it is easy for the rider to evade them for some reason or another. Patience is certainly the prime factor in the animal's education. Imbued with it, the trainer will be in a position to follow progressively the principles he understands, abiding by the rules he has learnt, which are, after all, self-evident.

PART TWO

CHAPTER TWO

Principles of Training for Movement on the Flat

The component factors in the training of a show jumper for his movements on the flat are free forward movement, obedience to hand and leg, balance, and impulsion. When a high degree of impulsion can be produced and maintained, a certain amount of natural collection will appear for a few seconds. I mean by this that a horse trained to this standard will instinctively gather himself to face an awkward situation, thereby producing collection for a few strides. But the collection is not enforced, and the horse is not moving forward at a collected canter ordered by the rider. He is merely developing, of his own accord, a shade more impulsion than that which the rider is capable of producing. It will therefore be a natural reflex action, and his physical attitude will not be similar to that required for periods of collected movement.

I am entirely opposed to the theory that a show jumper's training on the flat should be based on the search for collection. I maintain that the accuracy essential for success must come from complete education in the four component factors, resulting in rhythmical and fluent movement, which will always allow the horse's natural freedom and liberty to take effect. Any curtailment of freedom and liberty will restrict his ability to deal with awkward situations and can well sap his courage. The cry should always be 'Forward in control', so that when the take-off platform is reached the forward trend can be pursued in the form of forward propulsion into the air. This will mean that the rhythm and fluency of balanced movement during the approach will join forces with locomotion, to minimise the muscular effort required to make height and distance. The opposite of this, elevated impulsion, will call for a degree of enforced collection during approach, so that the forehand is lightened by each successive step prior to take-off, and the centre of gravity correspondingly moves back. In consequence, one small error of judgement on the rider's part, or a slight disobedience by the horse, will result in the horse being on the take-off platform in a physical state that makes the clearing of the obstacle difficult and sometimes wellnigh impossible.

To foster forwardness at all times and, as will be seen later, to assist in accurate stride control, I recommend that the horse's head carriage should be low and, for purposes of show jumping only, even slightly over-bent. During the approach, which means for the whole time spent in a show jumping round on the flat, the horse should resemble a compressed, slightly convex, spiral spring, the centre of his back being the highest point of the bend. If in such a state the loins, quarters, and hind legs, which are the propelling apparatus, and in this instance the back end of the spring, can sweep smoothly downwards and forwards under his centre, thereby producing power and stability. The front end of the spring, the neck and head, should also be bent downwards and forwards, thereby helping the back to round correctly, giving freedom and liberty to neck and shoulder, and obviating the evasive tendency of the head to come up with a change of contact of the bit in the mouth. When proceeding in this way the horse will have full and free use of all limbs and muscles, will be in a position to bounce off the ground from either a short or a long stride, and will automatically keep travelling forward. Vice versa, a high head carriage will produce a ewe-shaped neck. This will lead to a hollowing of the back and a consequent slackening of the loin muscles. The angle of the spine will then prevent the quarters and hind legs from sweeping under the horse, and all power and elasticity will vanish. Conformation, in the form of well-shaped shoulder and neck, and ample room in the jowl, can help greatly in the production of a low and constant head carriage.

THEIR EXECUTION: FREE FORWARD MOVEMENT

I always think that this is something of a misnomer. It is all very well to get going freely, but what about stopping? Accurate acceleration and deceleration is a better description of what is required. From the beginning, when a young horse is being lunged prior to backing, he will respond more easily to indications for acceleration than to those for deceleration, and this will usually be particularly conspicuous in an animal of high courage. But there is no reason at all why any type should not be educated to answer the lightest of impressions on the sensory nerves concerned. The horse to be considered in this context will have arrived at a standard of training in which he will understand what is meant by the rider, but will not necessarily answer correctly. So it is important that the trainer should always be strict about the quality of the horse's free forward movement, even when carrying out only routine exercise. For all subsequent movements, and the assimilation of the other component factors, obedience, balance, and impulsion are entirely dependent for their accuracy on this part of the training. The object must therefore be twofold; first to teach the horse to bring his hind quarters into operation to produce forward propulsion by a very light pressure of the rider's leg within a small area just behind the girth, and secondly to produce a withdrawing action of the head and neck, following through to the rest of the horse's body, by strengthening very slightly the pressure of the mouthpiece of the bit on that part, or parts, of the mouth upon which the bit in use is designed to work. In fact the horse should respond to 'the breath of a boot' and the touch of a finger. Obviously this cannot happen at once, but strict riding at all times can achieve it.

Work on straight lines, preferably with something solid, such as a thick hedge, on one side, call for a transition from, say, the walk to the trot by the application of a reasonably strong, but short-lived, leg pressure; if this is ignored, use the whip once, just behind the leg, on the side away from the hedge, or give a touch of both spurs. This will make the horse jump forward; move back into the walk again, and repeat the question with leg pressure only. Continual repetition with suitable reward will eventually produce the answer, but remember to give the head and neck freedom. In reverse try for a decrease of pace from, say, the trot to the walk by finger pressure on the reins; if this is ignored, set the outside hand, and increase strongly the contact with the other for a second, relax it, and increase it again. When this is successful, return to finger pressure only. Aim throughout for smooth, but instantaneous response, and keep the movement straight and the head low. When results are being obtained on level ground carry out the same exercises up and down hill and over undulating country. Vary also the pace within the different gaits except the walk, which should always be free, the stride being low and close to the ground. The trot, at whatever pace, should have a swinging tempo. As accuracy in free forward movement is being instilled into the horse he can also be taught to accept the bit as required by the rider.

During a show jumping round it is of paramount importance that the head carriage is in a constant position, as well as being low. The rider will not need to have throughout exactly the same feeling on the reins, and so the extent of contact will change. For instance, this will be an automatic part of his technique in stride control. Therefore the horse must be taught to accept contacts of different strengths without moving his head from its already low position. This can be practised on straight lines over varying types of country by proceeding for a few strides with a steady degree of contact, the next few with a lighter degree, and the next with a stronger again, keeping the same pace throughout. It is unnecessary, and can be injurious, to school the horse to be on the bit in the sense required for manège dressage. Suppleness and resilience must be encouraged, and control sought for over each coil of the spring. I cannot over-emphasise the importance of super-accurate free forward movement. The rider must always keep it in his mind and be emphatic that, whatever is happening, the horse's response is instantaneous, smooth, and accurate. He must, however, always remember that periods of relaxation are an essential part of training, and that loose rein work not only provides such relaxation, but is also valuable to the normal process of schooling.

OBEDIENCE TO HAND AND LEG

The teaching of one component factor overlaps and blends with the others. When dealing with free forward movement obviously the horse is learning to obey indications from hand and leg on straight lines and, at the same time, his balance will be improving. It is therefore reasonable for the rider to consider that he is, in fact, so far teaching the two things at the same time, and can keep note of his feel of the general state of balance without doing anything positive about it. But a show jumper—and he is no exception among horses—cannot always keep to a straight line, so the next step must be to introduce obedience to indications by one hand or leg, supported by the other. The main objective will be to carry out changes of direction correctly at varying speeds, so that at all times the hind feet follow in the track of the fore, the horse is bent towards the new direction and, in consequence, the predetermined track on the ground can be exactly followed. It is here that suppleness must be seriously considered; so that the spring can bend comfortably in a convex fashion, the horse's neck muscles, those along his back, and his spine, must be supple on a straight line. But, when changing direction, lateral suppleness will also be necessary from front to rear, so that the circumference of the change can be exactly covered by his body. It is true to say that there is no wrong movement, no resistance, which is not preceded by the contraction of the muscles of the neck. It is also a fact that all horses, to a slight extent from the structure of the spine at birth, and often through not very good primary schooling, are a little one-sided; they find it easier to bend one way than the other. Making the horse supple must therefore go hand in hand with making him obedient.

It can be taken as a general rule that in the main the rider controls the horse's hind quarters by the action of his legs, and the forehand by the action of his hands on the reins. Also that one leg or one hand acting in a positive rôle must have support from the leg or hand on the other side, so that the resultant movement taken by the horse is smooth, accurate, and in balance. The best primary lesson for obtaining response to a positive action by one leg is the turn on the forehand. Remembering that position must precede movement, choose a right-angled join of two walls or hedges, and position the horse along one wall with his head in the corner. Make certain that the horse is standing squarely on all four legs, and is accepting the bit lightly. To turn to the right, the head should be turned very slightly to the right, the quarters moved to the left by positive action by the rider's right leg, so that the off hind passes to the left in front of the near hind, and the whole horse pivots to the left on the off fore. Any tendency to rein back is anticipated and corrected by action with the rider's left leg. When progress is evident in a corner the exercise should be carried out along a straight wall or hedge, and eventually in the open. Obedience is primarily being obtained to the action of one leg, but the hand also comes into it to a lesser degree, and the whole process helps suppleness of neck and back. Continuing on the same theme, the shoulder in exercise is valuable, and is an introduction to a circular change of direction (Plate 14). To perform a right shoulder in, the horse's forehand is taken off the track to the right as if about to begin a circle. But instead of continuing with it the rider's right leg pushes the horse to the left, so that he will continue to go forward with the head, neck and spine describing a curve the centre of which is the rider's right leg. His left leg keeps the quarters on the track. A horse will at first find difficulty in bending his spine, and the exercise is best carried out at a trot. Straightforward open turns will need practice at the walk, trot, and different speeds of canter, with a variation in the degree of contact, and plenty of relaxation given with work on a loose rein, on country with different gradients. Here it is worth while to stress that it is an advantage to change the working site as much as is physically possible. A horse will soon become bored and disinclined to produce complete co-operation if always worked on the same small patch.

Curved changes of direction are the next logical step. Bearing in mind that accuracy in following the required route is dependent upon the hind feet following in the track of the fore, the shape of the horse's body must be similar to the shape of the curve. An eminent American writer has condemned as ruinous the bending of the spine to conform with the curve, on the ground that it will shorten the stride, and cramp and annoy the horse. I agree that the stride will be shortened but, unless practised, the show jumper's approach work will be catastrophic! Winning is an important point: so carry out half-circles, circles, and shallow serpentines at all paces. When cantering, vary the radius of the change and make large circles cantering false with the outside leg leading. This will lengthen and lower the stride, make the spine supple, lower the head and neck; and also may well be required when making a wide change of direction in the jumping arena. With a one-sided animal there will be difficulty in obtaining the desired curve, even with the strong use of a direct rein of opposition. There will also be the danger that, from continual strong pressure, the horse will become insensitive to the inside leg and continue to cut inwards in a barge-like fashion. I find that a circular track with a diameter of approximately fifty feet, and something solid or prickly just inside it, will help enormously to cure this serious fault (Plate 15). With the horse unable to make ground inwards, resistance will gradually lessen, the stiff muscles will regain elasticity, and accuracy in the open will follow. This easily built contrivance will also help to steady and quieten an excitable animal, all the time improving his balance. Different shades of contact are advised, including a loose rein. The rein back, apart from its practical value, serves three purposes. It is a 'suppling' exercise, one that requires obedience to combined hand and leg, and that greatly benefits balance. It can be introduced early in a horse's education, but progress in balance is necessary before it can be carried out accurately. It will be dealt with in the subsequent paragraph on that subject. It is of great importance to emphasise that the horse will expect and understand sensations and impressions from the rider's leg only in the small area behind the girth, in which the leg swings in rhythm with the horse's cadenced movements.

BALANCE

Balance is solely a matter of weight distribution. A horse is said to be balanced when his own weight and that of his rider is distributed over each leg in such proportion as to allow him to use himself with the maximum ease and efficiency at all paces. Balance is the essence of all riding. 'My horse got unbalanced', is an unarguable and complete answer to failure. The Derby has been lost by a fancied runner becoming unbalanced going down the hill at Epsom, and many a big show jumping prize has been lost by a horse getting into a similar state when moving away from the end of the arena. In specialised riding it is the quality of the balance that divides the mediocre from the high class. The horse, like the human being, has a natural balance. But, due to the addition of the rider's weight, and to the exigencies of practical exercises to be carried out in the pursuit of different branches of specialised riding, an artificial balance has to be created to make it possible for the horse to perform them correctly. This adds up to an appreciation of the ideal position for the centre of gravity of the mass for each separate occasion. This must vary very considerably. A 'flat' racehorse, who is only required to gallop, must sweep his hocks under him and will need his balance forward,

17. *Ridge and furrow country.*

18. *An oval loose jumping school.*

19. The figure-of-8 exercise, with small parallel fence at the centre of the '8'.

whereas a high school horse, whose main work is at collected gaits, with short periods of extension, will need to have it, in the main, far back.

What then of a show jumper? Broadly speaking the state of balance must alter with each variation of pace. Ideally a show jumping round is completed at a uniform pace. But fence construction, fence siting, and course design often enforce variations for purposes of examination. The show jumper must therefore acquire a balance which is adjustable (Plate 16). As can be seen from the horse's overall shape, the head and neck assume the rôle of balancer. When turned out, a horse will spend a great deal of his time grazing, with his head on the ground. But, if startled, he will immediately raise his head, not to pick out visually the source of the noise that has startled him, but to arrange his equilibrium for instant flight. Unfortunately, for economic reasons, and to take a short cut, the head of a young horse is often raised too rapidly by the use of the hand only, so that he can be passed on as a reasonable ride to the uninitiated. His eventual owner will then spend months, or even years, trying to get it down again!

This fault must always be avoided in a show jumper. With the spiral spring as a simile, its centre of gravity must be adjustable from front to rear and back again, without an upward trend at the front, by flexible forward and downward action directed at the back co-ordinated by backward elasticity in front. Such action will compress the spring, bend it in a convex fashion, and allow the centre of gravity to move forward or backward in ratio to the opening and shutting of its coils. When applied to a horse, the quarters and hind legs are pressed forward and downward, the head and neck, remaining low, are drawn softly slightly in, thereby maintaining the same pace, and rounding the back convexly. As a result the horse's paces will be springy and cadenced, and he will be in a state from which his centre of gravity can readily respond to adjustment. For most of the time this should be just forward of centre, allowing the propelling apparatus, the hind quarters, free scope. The result will of course be achieved by the dominance of the rider, but not by forcible means. With the establishment of mutual confidence, the desired ends can be obtained by firm suggestion applied through the horse's memory, without curbing his natural impulses and liberty.

The horse's intelligence, and the realisation that he must do

E

something to help himself, will produce a natural co-operation with the rider's suggestions when offered progressively difficult tasks in relation to the type of movement and the character of terrain. For instance, increase and decrease of pace across undulating country, such as wide ridge and furrow (Plate 17), will make the horse use his hind quarters of his own accord by bringing them under him, and stretching his head down and out. If he makes no effort to do this, he will sprawl and stumble. Freedom of head and neck must of course be allowed. By giving free scope to the horse's natural reactions to different situations and by superimposing his own light, but firm indications on the horse's inevitable muscular movements the rider can establish a subtle blend of confidence with his horse, and an inconspicuous and subconscious degree of dominance over him. The horse will, in this way, learn to obey automatically the finer shades of controlling technique.

In practice patience and simplicity must form the pattern. Top class fluid balance is elusive, and any attempts at short cuts to it will lead only to evasions and continual corrections of wrong movements. One cannot expect every horse to be a great mover, but limitations in conformation or breeding can be improved, though not transformed. Ideally, at the walk the strides should be long, free, and close to the ground; the trot should be low though springy, with feet moving close to the ground, with a swing of the back; and at a fast canter the feet should travel close to the ground, with little knee and hock action. For all types natural liberty must be encouraged and maintained. First lessons in suggestive balance should be given on the straight on a slightly downhill gradient if possible with, as always, a hedge or fence on one side to assist straightness. For a few strides at a time, followed by relaxation on a loose rein, urge the hind quarters forward with a sympathetic and rhythmical leg pressure. Fractionally after response to this, prevent increase of pace and draw the head and neck slightly inwards without raising, by giving an extra, but elastic feel to the mouth. Gradually, if the head at the start has been a trifle too low, the force from behind will bring it up to the required level. At the same time the animal will begin to resemble the desired spiral spring. Move then to uneven and undulating country, and spend much time riding across ridge and furrow when available.

When the quarters can be felt to be coming forward and under, and the hind legs engaging or working, carry out the same procedure in wide changes of direction and serpentines. The rein back exercise can then be introduced realistically. Remember that the horse should take distinct steps backwards and not shuffle, picking up each foot in sequence and putting it down again firmly. Decide, before starting, the number of steps to be completed. Four are always sufficient. Make things easy by selecting suitable ground, a footpath with fence on either side being ideal. Stand the horse alertly on all four feet with the head in the normal low position and, with the weight slightly forward to ensure loin and hind quarter freedom, relax active leg pressure and ask for backward movement by action of the fingers on the reins. Just before completion of the last step reverse the process, stand still for a second or two, and walk smoothly forward. As proficiency grows, incorporate the rein back into transitions through the gaits on a straight line, walk, trot, canter on named leg, trot, walk, halt, rein back, halt, walk and so on, both on even and undulating ground, all the time aiming at fluency of transition.

There will be many times in the jumping arena when it will be advantageous to gain momentum during the last stages of a change of direction. As an introduction to this, now and again increase the pace of the canter slightly during the last quarter of a half circle. It must never be forgotten that the search is for balance, and still better balance. The approach is the main problem, and it is in balance that the solution is to be found.

IMPULSION

It is a pleasant feeling to have something up your sleeve. Moral confidence makes for anticipatory and quick appraisal of a situation, however awkward it may be, and the knowledge of having something powerful and steadfast in support puts difficulties in their right and proper perspective. Impulsion fills the bill in this respect. Impulsion is the energy formed by the gathering and harnessing of the horse's forces of energy by the rider, and its presence is due to positive action by him. When produced he needs to take measures to hold it, so that it can properly fill the rôle of reserve force, in addition to perfecting the manoeuvre in operation at the time. It cannot be effectively and correctly produced until the animal has acquired a reasonable state of balance.

The processes in its production must be forward looking, and approached with tact and patience. Like balance, it cannot blossom in a day. Haste and impatience can spoil the sensitivity of the mouth, and so lessen obedience. I too often hear lack of impulsion put forward as the reason for failure in a young green horse, when the unfortunate animal is not yet in balance.

In effect, impulsion is generated when the spiral spring, in the shape of the horse's body, is compressed more tightly than is required for the state of balance necessary at the time. This allows for the release of sufficient energy for supporting action, without uncoiling the spring to the extent of disturbing balance. When the crisis for which impulsion has been called in strongly is passed, the spring must be recompressed and the original impulsion held for future developments. The creation of impulsion is therefore the natural, logical, and reasoned sequel to the acquisition of a balanced state. It is the aftermath to balance. As such its practical exploitation must follow the same lines as in the search for balance. But in this instance even greater care must be taken that the periods of persuasion towards it are of short duration, and that each period is followed by one of relaxation and reward on a loose rein. Again begin on straight lines, and on level and undulating ground, before going on to changes of direction. Gradually increase the period for which impulsion is held. Practise moving out of a change, keeping the same pace, increasing impulsion during the latter stages of the curve and holding it for four or five strides on the straight. Intersperse this with movement through the paces, including the rein back, but omitting the trot, and carry out large figures-of-8 trotting before changing the lead. I stress again, do not attempt to hold the spring at full compression for too long. The process calls for great muscular effort from the horse, and it is essential that the rider's imperceptible domination does not smother the horse's ambition and his zest for getting to the next goal which, for a show jumper, is the negotiation of the next fence. Above all, never confuse impulsion with speed. The two are poles apart, and bear no relation to one another.

All field dressage for the preparation for show jumping has, as its ultimate aim, precision. Precision in movement, precision in following the desired track, precision in stride arrangements, so that the horse arrives on the suitable take-off platform in the

20. *Jumping from one level to another.*

21. *Beginning to make a change of direction before landing.*

22. *The rider's position in relation to three angles. (See p. 88)*

23. *The fingers, with which the finest shades of controlling technique are achieved.*

most favourable way for his jumping ability to assert itself fluently and easily. Reasoned schooling in free forward movement, obedience, balance, and impulsion, with the accent always on forward liberty, will make precision possible, thus taking care of the approach, by far the most important department in show jumping. I have chosen to consider work on the flat before the development of the horse's jumping skill, for this reason. Show jumping entails coping with a succession of up to eighteen jumps in the space of about two minutes in a small area. This is made possible by accuracy during the whole approach; and stride arrangements within it can be practised, without detriment to actual jumping, by the use of poles on the ground. If these are placed to represent fences in a course, the horse can be exercised in the maintenance of balance and impulsion in following the desired track by accurate changes of direction, in variation of pace and so balance; and the rider can measure in his mind's eye where he would wish the take-off platform to be in front of each pole. He can then test the obedience he has hoped to create by making arrangements to dispose of unwanted fractions of a stride. He can also introduce the disposal method in which a slight bend of the head and neck towards the leading leg will shorten a little the overall length of the stride, ensuring meanwhile that the movement remains straight. With the exception of the shoulder in, I have not mentioned work on two tracks, which, in my opinion, is not necessary in a show jumper's education. The change at the canter will be considered in the next chapter.

E*

CHAPTER THREE

Development of the Horse's Jumping Skill

I am sure that horses like jumping. It gives them a thrill just as it does a man or woman. Now and again, I am equally sure, a famous jumper appears who goes beyond this—a horse who realises that his skill and prowess are being pitted in a trial of strength with the others, who knows that it is up to him to see them off and show the world that he is the horse of the day. A horse, in fact, who rises to the big occasion. But, being the exception rather than the rule, such a horse can be found only by pure chance. Nevertheless, real confidence between horse and rider, backed up by the horse's natural liking for jumping, may well lead to much the same thing.

Before embarking on the training of a horse for show jumping, I must assume that the trainer will have considered very carefully the horse's natural attributes, enumerated in a previous chapter. It is expensive and frustrating to fight against heavy odds, and most of those already mentioned are definite 'musts' if a horse is to have a reasonable chance of getting to the top. How best can the chosen animal's natural way of jumping be improved and developed to enable him to become a spectacular jumping machine? As balance is the essence of riding, so balance governs the jump. The jump is the one action in which a horse most markedly changes his balance and his attitude many times in the space of a few seconds. As the head and neck are basically the horse's balancer when moving on the flat, so are they the same during the jump. The direction taken by the head and neck will be followed by the rest of the body, and the extent of their extension will govern the freedom and resilience of all his other limbs. Stiff neck muscles will stiffen those in the back, and stiffness there will pass to the legs. The legs are then unable to fold, there will be no articulation of the knee and hock joints, the legs will remain nearly straight and, to clear the fence, the body will have to reach an extravagant height. The horse will in effect be hurling himself into the air, and that entails great effort. His natural cleverness, his subconscious feeling of self-preservation, and his desire to avoid mistakes, or even falls, will be destroyed by the fact that his balancing instincts and actions are retarded. Only a phenomenon can cope in this way with modern conditions, and it is very obviously quite the reverse to what is required.

A good natural jumper will show sense in his jumping. By this I mean that he will first take steps to produce himself in a state of spring or bounce immediately before take-off. Then, at take-off, and during the jump itself, he will contract or stretch his head and neck along the curved line in the air that will carry his whole body a sufficient height and width to clear the fence. He will be balancing himself and, to conserve effort, and as a result of being in balance, will fold his fore and hind legs under him. The extent to which he has to leave the ground is therefore reduced to a minimum. In fact, having prepared himself, the horse will describe a parabola in the air suitable for the size and construction of the obstacle. During the last two strides before take-off the horse will gather himself by lowering his head and neck, by sweeping his hind quarters forward and under, and by crouching for the spring to follow. This will be a natural and instinctive process. It will be the time when the rider should be giving the final help and encouragement before effacing himself from positive action during the jump itself. Having found and maintained suitable balance, having produced and held impulsion, the rider can release a fraction of it to assist the horse, and the horse will respond with a degree of natural and self-appointed collection. As the hind feet sweep forward to join the fore on the take-off platform, in order to move the centre of gravity slightly back and so assist the upward and forward propulsive effort, the horse will withdraw his head and neck a little.

This balance adjustment continues until the fore feet have just left the ground, when the sequence changes and the head and neck begin their stretching movement forward and upward, giving free play to the shoulder and fore legs. During the upward curve of the parabola the fore legs should fold and the weight continue its forward and upward trend. As the maximum height is reached by the fore hand, the head and neck increase the stretch to help the hind quarters up, and to allow complete flexion of the hocks, so that at the apex of the curve the fore hand is carrying the weight forward and downward, the back is rounded in the shape of the curve itself, and the hind legs are being tucked up to avoid danger. Then, coincidental with the fore legs touching the ground, the head and neck are slightly, very temporarily, withdrawn to move the weight back in preparation for further movement on the flat, while the hind legs unfold and stretch forward to adjust the whole mass to the normal free stride. The whole process is over and done with in a flash but, as I think will be seen, its success is achieved by balance. In consequence the use the horse makes of his head and neck during the jump is the most important factor. The development of his natural skill must therefore be based on perfecting it.

It is an undisputed fact that a horse with a natural spring, jumping loose, will seldom make a mistake. How often one has seen a faller at Aintree gaily skipping over the fences loose, making these very formidable obstacles look like hurdles. There are differences of opinion, however, about the value of loose jumping for educational purposes. My own opinion is that, from this aspect, time spent in planned loose jumping is seldom wasted (Plate 18). The anti-loose jumping school consider that it teaches the horse disobedience, because he alone can make arrangements during the approach, and will become accustomed to having his own way. This, they say, will result in resentment and resistance to the rider's dominant indications for stride control. On the other hand, loose jumping helps to develop and strengthen muscles used in the act of jumping; it improves balance, freedom, and liberty; it encourages the horse to make full use of his head and neck, round his back, and fold his legs. The horse can learn not to fear the action of the rider, so that, with no apprehension, he will be in a good frame of mind for the job. As a result of this his eye will be developed, enabling him to choose with precision the moment for take-off; he will thoroughly enjoy it, at the same time gaining confidence in himself and friendly respect for his rider's voice and character. Moreover no human being is infallible. Errors of judgement will occur, and the rider should reasonably expect the horse to lend a hand in avoiding trouble.

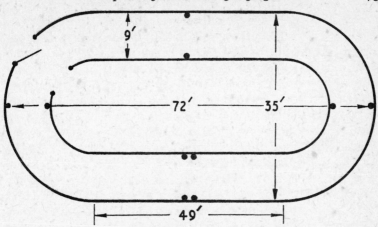

Fig. 5. Ground plan of loose jumping school

But loose jumping must be planned, and practised in a suitable place. The best method is to use an oval school or manège, 72 ft. in length, 35 ft. in width, with a 9-ft. track on the inside. This will allow for one jump on either side, and one at either end, which can be used as correctives to rushing. There will be room for an additional jump on the side to constitute a straight in and out, there will be space for three or four straight cantering strides from the end of a curve to take-off, and the horse will at all times be under the control of one man (Figure 5).

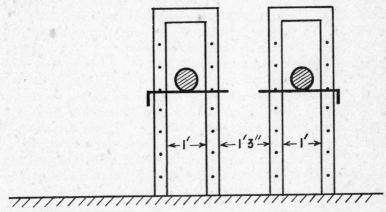

Fig. 6. Side view of parallel jump in loose jumping school

The ideal is to have the outside wall consisting of material that forms a screen, so that the attention of the horse cannot wander. Have an upright fence on one side and a parallel on the other, constructed of solid poles fixed on the same plane. Not being a believer in turning horses over for the fun of it, I like the poles to be capable of a 3 in. straight movement. If the fences are made in this way, the horse is given a chance of recovery after a bad mistake, without being able to disregard his error (Figure 6). A school of larger dimensions than this, allowing for more than one fence on the straight, will mean that one man cannot be in full control, and rushing can develop. For these reasons I am also entirely opposed to the use of straight lanes or corridors. For a good, trained jumper a larger school of non-uniform shape, with only short lengths of straight, can assist muscular development, and can accommodate such things as water or large ditches, but a school of this kind is costly, and needs much space (Figure 7). Lunging over fences is of value in the early stages of jumping training but, except with a very lazy horse, I am not in favour of it when further progress has been made. It can lead to a certain restriction of liberty, and it is difficult to keep the horse's undivided attention.

A horse in the state of jumping training that can be hoped for in a potential show jumper will probably have been schooled in the use of cavaletti. A cavaletto, Italian for 'little horse', is a jump in its simplest form—a rail on the ground. When supported at either end by small wooden crosses or blocks to variable heights up to about 18 in., it becomes a little wooden horse. Pieces of equipment like these are invaluable in the early stages of training, and remain so throughout the horse's jumping life. A series of cavaletti at their lowest height, spaced at 5 or 6 ft. from one another, and negotiated at a normal trot with evenness of gait and equanimity, will lower the horse's head and develop jumping muscles. A small fence can be added after the last cavaletto, the distance from it being varied. In this way the introduction to, and practice in, the regulation of the length of stride is supplied. Precision is the ultimate end, and this necessarily calls for such regulation. The horse's acclimatisation to them can therefore be coincidental with exercises for the development of jumping skill. A distance of 11 or 12 ft. will make a straight in and out; one of 22 to 24 ft. will allow for one non-jumping stride, while

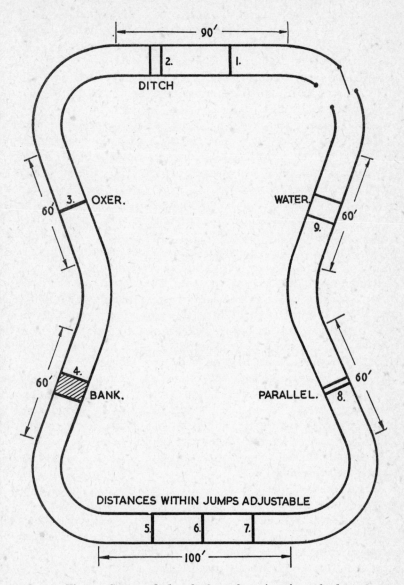

Fig. 7. Suggested plan for large loose jumping school

one of 31 to 33 ft. will allow for two. To make the jump easy the distances in the second and third instances will need to be varied according to the length of the horse's normal cantering stride. Small variations in distances will entail the lengthening or shortening of the non-jumping stride or strides to strike the required take-off platform. The horse's natural perception will spot this, and he will quickly become co-operative in the solution of disposal problems.

While the series of cavaletti are in use as the preamble, the first cantering stride will be after the last cavaletto. The number in the series can be gradually reduced to one, which can be approached at a slow, but relaxed canter. The remaining one should be at maximum height. It will be advantageous to use parallel poles for the fence in question, at first with, and later without, a ground line. This type of obstacle, which requires the making of both height and distance, will encourage the proper use of head and neck, the rounding of the back, and will induce the legs to fold. As an alternative, use a reversed triple bar which will call for a slightly steeper parabola, but which must still have width. The parallel fence can be up to a height of about 3 ft. 6 in., with a spread of about 4 ft. When using this type of guide to take-off, the objective on the flat is obedience by suggestion and persuasion, best achieved by a generally relaxed approach to the whole affair, maintaining balance, but without attempting marked impulsion. It will also lead very nicely to dealing with closely related fences in the shape of doubles and trebles. Moreover another important item in the overall plan can be introduced. In order not to waste time and to be in a position to treat the jumping of several consecutive fences as one operation, as well as to simplify the problem of maintaining balance and impulsion throughout, the horse must move off freely and boldly into his stride immediately after landing. If then there is any tendency on the part of the horse to dwell on landing, as there may well be, he will require a quiet urge forward as he begins the first stride away.

Bearing in mind the scope of the course builder in the siting of fences, jumping training should incorporate all situations that can arise. First there are the unrelated fences, which are sited at a distance of 80 ft. or more from each other, with and without a change of direction on the route between them. Jumps like these can be treated separately from the point of view of stride arrange-

24. Cantering on an upward gradient with the seat bones out of the saddle.

25. *The first part of the straight section of the approach, with seat bones just out of the saddle.*

26. *The seat bones in contact with the saddle for the last three or four strides before take-off.*

ment, but a uniform pace should be maintained, and care taken that movement after landing is free and bold. Bring in impulsion and, when coming out of a change of direction, do so with conviction and purpose so that the straight part of the approach shows zest and fluency. Use all the four available types of fence. Secondly, practise over related fences, which are sited in a straight line at distances between 80 ft. and 39 ft. 4 in. from each other. Here, success in jumping the second will be largely dependent upon action and consequent movement on landing over the first. Certain distances within the two limits will obviously suit the particular horse's normal stride, so that without interrupting the rhythm an even number of strides brings him on to the second take-off platform. Then change the distance slightly so that instead of there being, say, 5 even strides there are $5\frac{1}{8}$, or $4\frac{7}{8}$. The disposal of the unwanted fraction can be obtained by lengthening or shortening one or two strides somewhere between the two fences.

The horse's eye and instinct will help the rider's indications, but always make sure that he gets away freely after landing over the first fence. Any hesitation will quite clearly spell disaster ahead. The distances employed are largely a matter of trial and error for different horses, but bear in mind that the ideal take-off platform varies according to the type and structure of the fence. As a guide, a normal horse will meet fences correctly if they are spaced at 45, 55, 65, and 75 ft. from each other, measured inside to inside, on flat ground, and on good going. Be reasonable, and do not build very big fences. These related fences are very important indeed. In my opinion success in dealing with them easily and fluently, from the jumping angle, depends entirely on a completely free get-away after landing. If the horse makes this automatically whenever he lands, obedience and the maintenance of balance and impulsion will do the rest (Figure 8). Thirdly are closely related jumps, or those sited at 39 ft. 4 in. or less from each

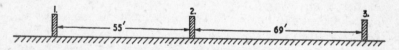

Fig. 8. Three related fences in line. An easy distance between 1 and 2.
A difficult distance between 2 and 3

other, constituting a double or treble fence. Such fences provide horse and rider with their greatest headache. All horses, whatever their ability and experience, regard doubles and trebles with a certain degree of apprehension. This is perfectly understandable. If a treble, constructed mainly of poles, is sited immediately after a sharp change of direction, the horse will suddenly face a sea of poles. Obviously one leap will not clear them, but he cannot see exactly where he can land among them, and his confidence may fade. The rider knows full well that, to get out at the far end, his arrangements up to the first fence must be bold and precise. A slight error will spell trouble. Apprehension is a very real danger. The solution is, of course, practice and still more practice. In view of all this the motto must be 'Easy does it'. Start therefore with a double, and make it as simple as possible, so that the horse will jump boldly in and get happily out at the other end. This will mean a solid, inviting type of jump for the first, one which encourages horse and rider to 'have a go' such as a low wall with a rail just beyond, or a low hedge with a pole beyond, to form two stairs of a staircase. Make the inside distance one to suit the particular horse's normal stride, and approach the fence with resolution, and impulsion to spare.

Vary the types of jumps, an upright in and a spread out, and vice versa. Also cater for two jumps of the same kind. Confidence must be established before difficulties are introduced; and they can be set in two different ways. First by the type of one jump in relation to the other, and secondly by the distance between them measured from the landing element of the first to the take-off element of the second, or inside to inside. A high upright followed by a spread presents one type of problem, a spread followed by an upright, another. Distances that make the non-jumping stride longer than normal, and those that make it shorter, are, again, different questions. A long distance calls for expenditure of impulsion on landing, and will be greatly assisted if the horse has learnt always to get away freely. A short one demands implicit obedience on landing and a high state of balance at take-off for the first jump. The permutations in the arrangement of both jumps and distances are considerable and should be treated with respect. It is remarkable how the difficulty increases in ratio to a few inches of distance. Very naturally one distance found simple by one horse will present problems to another of differing conformation and temperament. When schooling, therefore, start with measurements that suit the particular horse and, when real confidence is established, vary them a little either way. A guide to the most usually employed types of double is tabulated in Figure 9.

FIG. 9. EASY DISTANCES WITHIN COMBINATION FENCES

Type of combination	*1 non-jumping stride*	*2 non-jumping strides*
Two uprights	26 ft.	35 ft.
Two parallels	23 ft. 6 in.	34 ft.
Upright to parallel	24 ft. 6 in.	34 ft. 6 in.
Upright to staircase	24 ft.	34 ft.
Parallel to upright	26 ft.	36 ft.
Parallel to staircase	25 ft.	34 ft. 6 in.
Staircase to upright	26 ft.	35 ft. 6 in.
Staircase to parallel	25 ft.	35 ft.

Pyramid type jumps within combination fences can produce trick distances.

I am sure that it is right to jump little and often. But boredom breeds non-co-operation, and the more the jumping exercises can be varied the better, not only in the type of exercise, but also in the working site. A variation can be provided by the use of one fence, preferably parallel poles, 15 ft. in length, placed at the centre of a figure 8. Put at each end of the 8 a guide, such as an oil drum or fence stand. The distance from the fence to each drum should be a minimum of 90 ft. Proceed then to canter along the line of the 8 going round the drums and jumping the fence in the middle from either side. Many useful lessons are incorporated in the one exercise. Balance and impulsion must be maintained; accurate changes of direction must be carried out to either hand; stride arrangements can be practised; jumping a fence at a slight angle can be introduced; and the horse will learn to anticipate and perform the change of lead at the canter without a specific indication from the rider (Plate 19). This is an important asset. The show jumping rider has a great deal about which to think, and concentrate on, during a round. The change at the canter can take place only during the moment of suspension. This moment is of fractional duration, and the indication from the rider for it must therefore be exactly timed and exactly in rhythm with the movement. Any slight discrepancy in its application will merely upset balance, take the horse's mind off his job and will not have the desired effect. If the horse can learn to perform the change of his own accord when going into a fairly sharp change of direction, it is so much the better. Provided that balance is there, he will soon learn to change, if necessary, at the ends of the 8, mainly because, by doing so, his own situation will be made easier. This is, of course, certainly contrary to the ethics of manège dressage, in which anticipation by the horse is anathema. But, for show jumping, simplify where possible; this is an occasion in which to do so. A balanced horse will be happy and relaxed on a wide half-circle, leading with the outside leg. But, as his head, neck and spine begin to bend sharply, he will know what is happening and will react accordingly.

So far emphasis has been laid on educating the horse in jumping either isolated, or groups of isolated, fences. As progress is made in each, consideration should be given to welding the groups together with a view to taking on a complete course. A rectangular piece of flat ground, in the region of 100 yds. by 75, will serve the purpose. Mark each corner with a guide post and site five jumps in the centre, two comprising a one stride double fence, as shown in Figure 10. It will be seen that three of the jumps are of parallel variety. It should be possible to jump them all from either side. Taking the four corner posts as guides to the area in which to work, a route can be planned in which eight fences are jumped in succession, each one preceded by a change of direction. The aim should be to maintain fluency and, to be a little Irish, move with relaxed animation. Any tendency to boil up should be corrected by proceeding round the rectangle at a trot or canter on a loose rein. Then, to go a little further, choose the corner of a field, so that two sides of the rectangle are enclosed. Place the fences as before, but add another to be jumped after having rounded the enclosed corner. Here the lessons will be the same, but will include making full use of available ground space on the two sides bounded by hedges, and the production of impulsion for the additional fence out of the corner. In fact exact accuracy in following the

27. *The take-off. First stage.*

28. *The take-off. Final stage. Myself schooling at Weedon for the Olympic Games of 1936.*

29. *The airborne period. An early stage. Captain Raimondo d'Inzeo on 'The Quiet Man' at Aachen.*

30. *The airborne period. A stage later. Captain Raimondo d'Inzeo on 'The Quiet Man' at Aachen.*

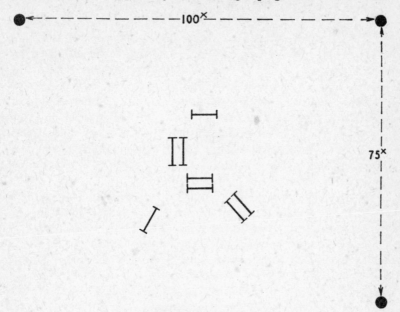

Fig. 10. *Plan of rectangular jumping manège*

planned track can be tested and practised. Human ingenuity will of course provide many different designs for the siting of fences and, provided that a uniform pace can be maintained throughout, the more variations there are, the better.

There are fences, other than the ordinary types, which must be tackled. Banks are a feature of some international arenas. If a bank proper is not available, jumping from one level to another will help (Plate 20). The horse must be thoroughly acquainted with ditches of all types, whether holding water or not, so that there is no hesitation, and its limits become merely useful guides to the position of the take-off platform. Last but not least, there is the bogey of the show jumping ring—the water jump. On the face of it a horse should have no difficulty whatsoever in clearing a mere 14 ft. of water. Yet, certainly in Britain, faults still tend to mount up when a fair-sized water is included in the course. With more shows providing water during the past few years, the situation has improved, but difficulty in finding schooling facilities is no doubt the main reason for there being any

F

water problem. It is, in fact, another type of fence that brings some apprehension, but the horse may soon discover that the water has no depth, and landing in the far edge causes no discomfort! Once he has become entirely accustomed to water as merely another obstacle in his path a bold horse will have no problem, always provided that his rider fully understands that water must be treated as a flat, wide, pyramid jump, that it must be approached with great impulsion and a crescendo of momentum, and that the take-off platform must be close up against the guard fence. A mad gallop will achieve nothing. One must gain height to achieve distance.

Finally, before embarking on a complete show jumping course, consideration must be given to time as the deciding factor. As I have indicated, progress in this country was retarded by the delay in bringing the time element into the rules. This was no doubt largely due to misconceptions about the right methods for beating the clock. An apparently leisurely performance defeats 'fits and starts' of rushing, stopping and galloping. It is the track taken, the angle at which the fences are approached and jumped, the quick balanced get-away on landing, the horse's suppleness and, above all, the fluency of movement throughout the round, which decide the issue. The normal round should flow; one against the clock should call to mind an unhurried flood. Its achievement will merely be the acme of field dressage. All stages and details of training have had as their goal the assurance of the horse being able to complete a course, however twisting, in a balanced state and at an even pace, fluently and smoothly. Basically the horse is being educated to 'turn on the tap' when he has had sufficient ring experience, and the rider must decide when this moment has arrived. It will not have arrived until he is equally at home jumping from a long or short stride after a short straight approach, and until he has acquired calm in the ring. There are several methods for the preparation of the horse. Implement 'suppling' and obedience training by making acute changes of direction between two fences, keeping the same pace. To facilitate this, and to assist in the maintenance of impulsion, swing round the bend, making a little ground away from the second fence. Move past a fence at a good round pace, and swing back to jump it. Practise jumping fences in the corner, as near the fence stand as possible, and approach jumps, other than spreads, at an angle.

This will have been done when carrying out the figure 8 exercise. It will also be advantageous to give schooling in the technique of beginning a change of direction in the air before landing. The success of this manoeuvre will be in the rider's hands. Fractionally after the horse has topped the fence, the rider will need to bend the horse's head and neck towards the new direction, at the same time distributing his own weight towards the bend (Plate 21). The horse will then be moving towards the required direction as he lands. The old cry that it is criminal to race a good horse is a fallacy. An intelligent approach to the time problem will benefit a horse rather than harm him.

I have always found that a horse trained on these lines will develop into a high-class show jumper if his natural attributes stand up to the ultimate test—ring performance. It can, unfortunately, be otherwise. Disappointments in any specialised subject, such as show jumping, are bound to occur. But a horse trained for show jumping who, in the end, does not really like the game, will be a brilliant hunter. I mention this fact because I know that the suggestions I have made for educating horses on the flat and over fences are applicable to any horse that is to jump first or last in the hunting field, and many of the suggestions can be beneficial to the training of steeplechasers.

CHAPTER FOUR

The Rider

POSITION AND TECHNIQUES OF CONTROL ON THE FLAT

Shakespeare aptly said that 'all the world's a stage, and all the men and women merely players'. The rider who wishes to become a specialised horseman must move out of the ruck of players and assume the rôle of producer. To reach this pre-eminent position he will have to be assured of the necessary knowledge, and of his technical ability to impart that knowledge to the player, his horse. Consideration has been given to the first two of the three decisive factors for success. It remains then to analyse the third, the rider's position or attitude on the horse's back at all paces and during the jump and, as a result of this, the methods he is able to employ to impart his knowledge to the horse. The beginner has only two objectives, to remain on the horse, and to control him. The specialised horseman takes over from there, and aims at perfecting both systems.

During this century many different theories concerning the rider's seat, or position, in the saddle have been advanced. We have had the English hunting seat, the Caprilli or Italian forward seat, the McTaggart forward seat, the Balanced seat, the Dressage seat, and no doubt many others. Since 1900 there has certainly been a revolution in the ways and means of riding but, whatever type of position is adopted, there is general agreement that it must be based on security; so that the bits and pieces of the human frame which are logically used for controlling the horse are entirely independent of those affecting security. A firm and independent seat fulfils this, and is the foundation of good riding. It is generally accepted that security is achieved by the blending of grip, balance and suppleness, that grip should be applied as required on the saddle down the inside of the thigh to, and inclusive of, the knee; that the rider's balance on the horse is maintained by the distribution of the weight of his trunk to conform with the horse's movements, assisted by springiness and pressure on the stirrup irons; and that suppleness all over his anatomy makes balance possible. When security has been achieved by the proper functioning of these three things, it leaves free for other uses the rider's instruments for control, his lower legs and feet, and his arms, wrists, hands and fingers. The rider will wish in the end to appear to be placed naturally on the horse, to be part of him, to be relaxed, but tidy, and to be in a position from which he can communicate his requirements clearly and firmly, at all times being in harmony and rhythm with the animal's every movement.

Major Piero Santini, an Italian cavalryman and a disciple of Caprilli, wrote in 1932 that 'the verb "to sit" should be eliminated from our vocabulary where riding is concerned'. He followed this up by observing that 'nothing gives a greater impression of lack of style and *chic* in a horseman than using the saddle as he would the family armchair'. Certainly the word 'sitting' gives a somewhat cumbersome and final impression, but its opposite, 'perching', conjures up thoughts of remoteness, and the rider should certainly not be remote from his horse. The answer is, I think, that the English language provides no alternative to the verb 'to sit', and that, in a riding context, sitting does not imply the imposition of dead weight, but contact with the centre of the saddle whereby full scope is given for the employment of the rider's instruments of control, and for adjustment to the overall centre of gravity. No two people have exactly the same build. To some *chic* and style come naturally. For others the enforcement of an unnatural position just to make them look stylish will only bring stiffness, thus diminishing the efficiency of their control. The aim must obviously be to arrive at a workmanlike, relaxed, forward seat, which will benefit horse and rider alike. A good position is not derived only from elegance. It is one from which the rider will be able to control his horse effectively.

SADDLES

There are innumerable different makes of saddle on the market.

There are some that, by their shape and construction, tend to cramp and restrict the rider to the extent of rigidity of action. These should be avoided. Choose one that, above all, fits and is comfortable. To fit well, the flaps must be rounded sufficiently far forward to ensure that the knees are well on them when the leathers are the right length, bringing the thigh and tibia to the proper angle in relation to one another. It must be remembered that the spring of the horse's ribs affects his shape under the saddle, and so the length of stirrup. To be comfortable, a saddle needs a fairly broad, well-defined centre, on to which the rider's seat bones automatically go when he lowers himself on to the saddle. The extent of the curve in the seat of the saddle will clearly define the centre and prevent the centre of gravity from slipping back. An exaggerated tilt of the cantle will, however, produce stiffness in the back. A knee roll is purely and simply an artificial aid. Thicker padding in the under part of the saddle, in front of where the rider might want to rest the knee, is preferable to a thick roll on the outside of the flap. The latter can well dictate the length of leather used, which should be done by the horse's conformation and the type of riding being practised.

POSITION

The rider's position should be rendered secure by his placing different parts of his anatomy at various angles in relation to each other. When the seat bones are resting on the saddle, either when the horse is stationary or moving, they must not deviate from its centre. Details of position can best be considered by starting at the lowest level. The heel must be down and the toe up. This brings the knee up against the saddle flap, placing the thigh against it, and forms approximately a right angle between thigh and tibia. The knee, pressing inwards, forwards and downwards, should become the immovable hinge of all action. The fact that the heel is down will enable the muscles inside the thigh to engage, producing grip in anticipation of such grip being required, and will bring the lower leg into a natural position in relation to the thigh, behind the perpendicular. The outward angle of the foot must be a natural one, and the knee and ankle joints must be supple, so that the lower leg can move within prescribed limits. From the hip joints upwards, the body should follow the move-

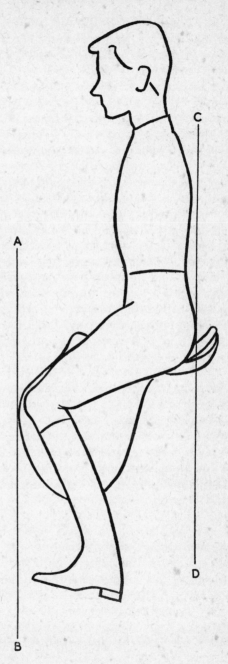

Fig. 11. *The sitting position*

ments of the horse and be slightly forward of the perpendicular, with the back straight, but never intentionally hollowed. Placed in this way, the rider will have acquired a sitting position formed by three angles, in the ankle, knee, and hip joints (Figure 11). The toes should not at any time move forward of the perpendicular line AB, or any part of the body, heels included, behind CD.

It is of paramount importance that all joints are supple. Balance must then come in, for it is the governing factor in security. It must be made possible by suppleness, backed up by springiness, and assisted by grip when required. Balance is the adjustment of the rider's weight, with the exception of his arms, upwards of the hip joint when sitting, and of the knee when the seat bones are out of the saddle, to conform with every movement of the horse. Springiness produces harmony in the conformity, and emanates from suppleness in the three joints forming the angles, with particular reference to flexibility of the ankle and pressure on the stirrup. A man sitting in an angular position in a chair has no spring in his body with his feet off the ground. But, when they are on the ground, he has the same type of spring as when standing on his feet. When riding, the stirrups are the artificial substitute for the ground. A straight, erect, fixed body has no spring in it, and cannot therefore have good balance. The quick and sudden movements of the horse produce shocks which the rider must absorb. The flexibility of his joints acts as a shock absorber. The knee, although its contact in one place with the saddle flap should be permanent, must not keep a fixed, rigid grip. It must always retain its elasticity so that its function as a hinge is always available. Above all the rider must be relaxed and natural, with no muscle in use except for a specific purpose (Plate 22). Photogenic attitudes compromise both security and control.

HANDS

The word 'hand' denotes the whole of it, the fist, and suggests bulk and force. In riding, 'hands' implies primarily the use of two sets of four fingers and thumb, and these should resemble those of a pianist or violinist in suppleness and sensitivity. It stands to reason that security directly contributes to lightness of hand, but it is also true to say that suppleness and sensitivity of fingers and wrist can be a natural gift—hence, no doubt, the much used axiom that 'good hands are born, not made'. Obviously the fingers cannot compete on their own, but are supported by use of the wrist, forearm and upper arm. Again, very obviously, none of these must have any connection with security. Following the important principle that no muscle in the rider's anatomy must be in use except for a specific purpose, the rider's forearm and hands must be placed normally, with the forearm brought up to form an angle with the upper, so that the reins can rest in the fingers which, of their own accord, are slightly flexed. The only muscle in use is one under the forearm to conteract the force of gravity. The forearm will naturally come up a shade obliquely towards the horse's neck, and the knuckles will be turned outwards and approximately half upwards. As long as there is no enforcement or constraint, the hand is then in a relaxed attitude, ready for positive action. Shades of tension can then be applied to the reins which, through the mouthpiece of the bit, give different feeling or sensations to the sensory nerves in the bars, lips or tongue, or to a combination of the three. The feeling can be straight, or inclined laterally. First it is produced by folding the fingers to the fullest extent towards the palm; secondly by flexion of the wrist, and thirdly by withdrawal of the forearm. The three can act alone or concurrently. The fingers are the crux of the matter. Each finger of each hand should be capable of separate movement, giving subtle variations of feeling. Moreover, there is nothing quicker or stronger than the fingers if properly employed. It is with them that the finest shades of controlling technique are achieved (Plate 23).

ACTION OF HANDS AND LEGS

Rhythm holds a position in riding second only to balance. A high-class ballroom dancer will have no difficulty in finding partners to follow his most intricate steps, and a rider blessed in this way will obtain immediate and willing response from his horse. Not only will he be an unobtrusive foil to his horse's every movement, but also the interdependence of the use of his hand and leg will translate his aids into indications addressing the horse's intelligence, and not into material means of constraint. The use of the lower leg is confined to an area to comply with the system of association of sensations, which coincides with the arc through which it will freely swing behind its normal position in rhythm with the three-time canter, with its limits the line CD in Figure 11. The knee performs its function as a hinge, and the heel must be down. The hands on the reins have a far wider range. The reins act by the mouth on the head, the neck, and the shoulder. In addition to having an ordinary give and take forward and backward action, they enable the rider to place the head in relation to the neck, the neck in relation to the shoulder, and the shoulder in relation to the quarters. They can even act indirectly on the quarters by giving to the shoulder a position which obliges the quarters to change.their direction. They can therefore oppose the shoulder to the quarters. These different results depend upon the tension given to the rein, and upon the direction in which such tension is applied. As a matter of convenience the action of one hand, supported by the other, can be grouped under five headings, though there are numberless intermediate actions between these five. In Figure 12 M represents the horse's mouth. R represents the rider in the saddle, and X and Y represent the practical angle of application of the direct and indirect reins respectively. The five headings shown in the diagram are:

    A. The direct rein.
    B. The direct rein of opposition.
    C. The indirect rein.
    D. The indirect rein of opposition in front of the withers.
    E. The indirect rein of opposition behind the withers.

A rein of opposition implies that a backward tension is exerted on the rein. In the direct and indirect reins there is only a lateral tension. Of these headings A and B are the reins continually used, and it will be as well to have a clear understanding of their methods of use, and the reasons for the consequent results.

A. *The Right Direct Rein*

The head is turned to the right followed by the neck and shoulder as tension increases. The weight of the head and neck is carried on to the off shoulder. If stationary, the horse will turn to the right on his centre. If the left leg is applied more strongly, he will turn on his haunches.

If in movement, with an equal pressure of both legs, he will

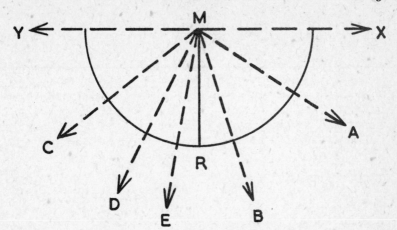

Fig. 12. *A. The direct rein. B. The direct rein of opposition. C. The indirect rein. D. The indirect rein of opposition in front of the withers. E. The indirect rein of opposition behind the withers*

make a large turn to the right, hind feet following in the track of the fore.

B. *The Right Direct Rein of Opposition*

By giving the right direct rein a backward tension the horse's right shoulder is drawn backward, and the weight of the head and neck thrown on to it, so as to oppose it to the quarters which are forced to the left.

If stationary, the horse will turn to his right on his centre or forehand, reining back as he does it, the quarters being forced to the left.

If in movement, the horse will slacken pace, and the stride of the off fore will be shortened. The horse will make a sharp turn to the right, the hind feet following outside the track of the fore.

The right leg should exert the stronger pressure so as not to have opposing aids. The technique of control is thus based on the sympathetic combination of pressures produced by the hand and leg. When the seat is secure they can be used together, or separately, one from the others. To achieve the full measure of accuracy with lightness, each component part of the communication system, down to each separate finger, needs to be supple, and to be attuned to the horse's sensitivity and mental make-up. It is a human trait that if one part of the body moves in a certain direction, the corresponding part on the other side moves in the same direction in sympathy with it. The two hands are instances of this. In order to obviate this tendency, it is advisable to ride with the hands well separated.

CONTROL OF MOVEMENT ON THE FLAT

The exercises and requirements for the horse's education on the flat, as described in Chapter 2, Part II, are very naturally dependent for their success on the adept blending of the use of the rider's hands and legs, and of his position on the horse's back for each one. The whole thing is a matter of feel and anticipation by the rider. In the end he must be the dominant figure. But his dominance needs to be accepted happily by the horse, without in any way crushing his initiative, his liberty, or his general zest for the job in hand. Broadly speaking, the rider has to consider four main factors—pace control, balance, changing of direction, and impulsion. In all these things he has to ensure that his horse is moulded into the guise of a curved, compressed, spiral spring, and that, when this state has been achieved, he can hold it with sympathetic dominance. This will lead him to short periods when he has to direct stride control, which will be discussed in the following chapter. Pace control derives from free forward movement and obedience. If these two basic factors of education have been quietly but firmly instilled, the rider can obtain graduated transitions of pace at the canter by the sole use of fingers and light leg pressure, the latter, of course, for all movements, slightly preceding the former. The maintenance of balance follows the same plan. Here, by the feel of the quarters, the rider must anticipate any tendency they may suddenly show of lagging behind and must urge the back of the spring forward with extra leg pressure. A constant low head carriage is also sustained by pressure behind, and often a slight sliding of the mouthpiece of the snaffle, or the bridoon of a double bridle, through the mouth will help towards it. It is obvious that when the rider's seat bones are in contact with the saddle he will be in the best position for exerting maximum leg effect. But, in this position, even when in perfect balance with his horse, there is slight restriction of natural liberty.

Except when the situation does, or may, demand maximum power and assistance from the rider, the best attitude for him to adopt is therefore one in which his seat bones are just out of the saddle; his balance is maintained by flexibility upwards of the knee, and by making full use of the stirrup with the heel well down, his hands remaining independent (Plate 24).

When changing direction the rider's main consideration must be to follow exactly the route he has chosen beforehand. But, however well trained his horse may be, there will be moments in a show jumping round when he will anticipate a new direction and try to cut inwards. It can in fact happen each time the track leaves the end of the arena. Intelligent use of the direct rein of opposition just before beginning the change will prevent evasion by the shoulder and quarters, the planned track can be followed, and the horse will himself change the lead if necessary. During a wide and long change of direction the rider has a golden opportunity to check on available impulsion, because he will almost certainly require something in hand to deal with the next fence. It will therefore help to swing into the curve, correctly bent, and to let the seat bones into the saddle for a few strides, so that proper compression of the spring can be assured. As with balance, it is the harmonious manipulation of finger and leg pressures that will first make impulsion a reality and secondly enable the rider to store it for use in emergency. With the time factor now universally adopted as a decider it is important for the rider to be a good judge of pace. With the help of a stop-watch, and a planned course design with guide posts instead of fences, this can very easily be practised on any reasonably flat piece of ground. The aim should be, in the first place, to acquire a steady and uniform pace to give time in hand over distances up to 1,000 yds. at 436 yds. per minute, the fastest of the speeds laid down for the initial stages of normal events. In the second, over shorter distances up to 600 yds., a faster overall time can be aimed at, following the principles discussed in Chapter 3.

Position is the foundation of harmony—harmony brings rhythm, understanding and confidence. With these established, the final stage, with the fences added as obstacles in the rider's path, can be tackled with assurance.

PART TWO

CHAPTER FIVE

Jumping the Round

The division of a show jumping round into phases greatly sim-
plifies the rider's appreciation of what he should or should not be
doing at different moments. Often a slight error at one stage will
follow through to the next, having repercussions resulting in a
definite fault being made. This can go further; for instance, a
fault that occurs when landing can often be traced to an error
made before take-off. It is the cause that requires investigation
and correction. Without the cause there will be no fault. The
rider needs therefore to be able to detach, visually and mentally,
each phase from the others, so that he can more easily pinpoint
the cause before its effect. The five suggested phases, as previously
mentioned, are the approach, take-off, over the fence, landing,
and get-away after landing. There are two factors common to all
five which the rider must always have in mind. First, assistance to
the horse and, secondly, control over him. I propose therefore to
take each phase separately and shall endeavour to elucidate,
simply, the main points to be watched in each.

THE APPROACH

The approach consists of all the time spent on the flat from before
passing through the start until just after passing through the finish.
So, as courses cannot be in one straight line, it automatically sub-
divides itself into two stages, a crooked part and a straight part.
The general track to be followed throughout is dictated by the
course design, which therefore depicts the radius of changes of
direction. The actual track taken must be chosen by the rider
when inspecting the course on foot. His objective must be to
simplify it by making full use of available ground space, and by
choosing the spot where the curve ends and the straight part

begins, which itself is governed by the size and difficulty of
the fence and by the siting of it in relation to available space.
The crooked or curved part can then be considered as a period of
preparation for the straight part, when any stride arrangements
necessary will have to be made. In the case of unrelated fences in
line the period from landing over one to a point 80 ft. from the
next will fill the same rôle. The ideal approach is unhurried,
calm, smooth and fluent. All work done in training on the flat has,
in a show jumper, this picture in view. The result—precision at the
speed required—is dependent on accuracy, arising from obedience,
balance and impulsion. The accurate riding of a particular course
is achieved by following exactly the chosen track in such a state,
which lays emphasis on the time allowed the rider to inspect the
course on foot, which will be considered in a later chapter. The
preparation period has been discussed in control of movement on
the flat. On a properly trained horse the rider should be able to
have his seat bones just out of the saddle throughout this period,
and continue in this way for the first section of the next (Plate 25).
During the next or straight period, anything that has started to go
amiss will develop into factual error, increasing in severity as the
fence gets nearer. The last two to four strides from take-off are
therefore the greatest danger time and, even if all seems well,
things can still go wrong. Therefore, during this last stage of
movement on the flat the rider must lower his seat bones to
contact the centre of the saddle, in order to be in a position of
maximum strength (Plate 26).

Leaving the matter of stride control to be dealt with as a subject on its own, there is another important approach matter. The
word 'attack', used in the 'twenties to apply to the approach to
a fence, has been in vogue again since 1952. It is employed to
describe the right method to adopt for the straight part of the
approach, and is applicable to the negotiation of difficult fences.
It implies simply and solely the expenditure of great impulsion
and resolution. It has no connection whatsoever with pace. As a
forerunner to it is the fact that it is imperative for the rider to
come out of any change of direction with conviction, and no loss
of momentum. Leaving the end of a small arena is a typical
example. But the essence of approach work is the field dressage
which must be planned and carried out beforehand, and continually practised with the most experienced of jumpers. The

approach is the crux of the whole matter. Accuracy and fluency of approach not only win, but also make for a stylish, gay and attractive display.

THE TAKE-OFF

During the approach the rider will have assisted the horse by following the route from which (and by keeping him in a physical state through which) he will be able to jump the fence easily and without undue effort. The climax will be reached when the horse's fore feet, followed by the hind, strike the suitable take-off platform. The take-off then begins, and again assistance and control are the two considerations. The take-off occupies a very short period of time. Just before, and for a fraction of a second after, the fore feet leave the ground, the horse, as has been said, will slightly withdraw his head and neck, preparatory to stretching them forwards and upwards to reach for height and distance. The rider therefore assists the horse in two ways. First he keeps an even feeling through the reins on the horse's mouth by following exactly the line the mouth takes. He thereby helps to retain the balance arrived at immediately before take-off. Secondly, he adopts a policy of non-interference, whereby he adjusts his weight to conform with the new upward thrust the horse is making. This entails a forward bend of the trunk from the hips, the extent of the bend being governed by the angle of the parabola the horse is beginning to describe, which itself is governed by the size and structure of the fence. The back should not be intentionally hollowed, and the rider should look ahead along the horse's crest. There must be no pivoting round the knee or stirrup iron. Control will be maintained by keeping the even feeling, already mentioned, on the horse's mouth, the hands following the line taken by the mouth; and so, as it moves away, they need to be separated to pass each side of the crest. The lower leg must remain in the same place in relation to the horse's side, with the heel right down. The seat bones will automatically leave the saddle as take-off starts so that the angle between thigh and tibia increases; but the increase must be made by the thigh from the knee as hinge, and not by any deliberate movement of the lower leg (Plates 27 and 28). A large majority of faults that occur in jumping have causes which can be traced back to the riders' errors during the moments just

31. *The landing. With all danger passed, the seat bones contact the saddle just before the hind legs reach the ground.*

32. *The landing. A fraction of a second later.*

33. *The beginning of the first stride after landing.*

34. *The first stride after landing nearing completion.*

before, on, and just after take-off. It is a vital part of the jump, but suppleness, correct lower leg position, and sympathetic hands will see it through. It must never be forgotten that unless the horse knows where the rider's hand is, he will never trust it.

OVER THE FENCE

This is the time when the majority of photographs of horses jumping are taken. No doubt such photographs make the best pictures, but they are not as valuable for instructional purposes as those of take-off or landing. If all has gone according to plan during the take-off, all should continue to be well while the horse is airborn over the fence. In Chapter 3 the horse's own balancing arrangements during this phase were described. The rider, being fully aware therefore of what he hopes will be happening under him, continues to assist with his hands by following exactly the line the mouth takes in the air, and with his non-interference policy by adjusting his own weight, again from the hips with knee as hinge, to preserve the overall balance and to be in balance himself. As the steepness and size of the parabola increase, so the horse will make more use of his head and neck. The hands then must be sufficiently separated to pass freely forward either side of the neck. In no circumstances must any additional weight be placed on the loins: the rider's weight must be forward, with the seat bones just out of the saddle until the hind legs are clear of the fence. A position of control must be maintained, with the lower leg again in the same position in relation to the horse's side, with heel down, and the hands acting as described above. The rider should be looking forward along the route he is about to take after landing, and his whole attitude should be relaxed and supple, with no trace of stiffness in the back or joints (Plates 29 and 30). Positive control can start during the latter half of this phase for the purpose of beginning a change of direction in the air before landing.

THE LANDING

The landing, similar to the take-off, occupies a very short space of time. At this stage assistance within the jump is nearly completed and control becomes positive as the horse's hind feet reach the

G

ground. Until just before the fore feet touch the earth, the danger of hitting the fence with the hind feet remains. To avoid this, still more use of the head and neck can be encouraged by offering a shade more rein with the fingers. In any event, of course, the same feeling should be maintained on the horse's mouth, as balance will be all-important a second later. As danger behind passes, the rider can begin to adjust his weight back, so that the seat bones are in contact with the saddle as the horse's hind feet touch the ground. From the control angle it is imperative that the lower leg remains in its proper place, with the heel down as always, that contact is maintained, and that the rider is looking forward along the track he will take in a second's time (Plates 31 and 32).

THE GET-AWAY AFTER LANDING

The rider may well experience a slight feeling of relief after the successful negotiation of a particularly difficult fence; concentration may then lapse, and things can start to go wrong. The first two or three strides immediately after landing are of vital importance within related and closely related fences, and although this phase is not in fact part of the jump itself, it is as well to separate it from the next part of the approach. To cope with problems ahead, it is necessary for the horse to move off in his stride after landing, in the same state of balance as that at take-off, without any signs of dwelling. This will have been encouraged throughout his jumping training, but it is important that the rider assists and is in a position for positive control. As the hind feet come to the ground his seat bones contact the saddle. Simultaneously extra leg pressure should be applied to produce thrust from quarters and hind legs. As the fore legs reach forward to make the first stride, the seat bones should leave the saddle again to allow the propelling apparatus freedom to sweep forward. The hands must keep the degree of contact required for the current situation. As always, the rider must look up along the chosen track. The importance of this short moment cannot be over-emphasised. I have already said that the successful negotiation of the second of two related or closely related fences is, in the main, dependent upon what happens at this stage. It is, in fact, a matter of common-sense and it puts paid to highly unorthodox or acrobatic positions over the fence. A properly trained horse will react automatically in the desired way on landing, and will need only a slight urge when a situation of great difficulty lies ahead (Plates 33 and 34).

STRIDE CONTROL

Stride control is the practical system whereby disposal is made of unwanted fractions of a normal stride existing within related and closely related fences, owing to the distance from point of landing to take-off platform not coinciding with an even number of such strides. Provided that the same pace is maintained, there can, mathematically, be only $\frac{1}{2}$ a stride to be disposed of—4 plus $\frac{3}{4}$ strides is the same thing as 5 minus $\frac{1}{4}$. Fractions can be disposed of by either shortening or lengthening one or more of the remaining normal lengthed strides; of the two, shortening is the more favoured. The main reasons for this are that it is the easier way, that psychologically it seems to give time for further consideration of the situation, and that it is the natural corollary to caution, and sometimes therefore to great fame. In fact, if properly executed, it adds greatly to propulsive power. If badly executed and, through indecision, practised consecutively to excess, shortening can grow into a running sore, and become the most disastrous of show jumping mistakes.

When shortening, the most important consideration is to maintain the same pace. Next, the head carriage must remain constant so that the back can be further rounded, allowing the hind quarters to move freely forward under the horse's body. A stride is shortened when its overall length is decreased from normal by the fore legs, with the hind legs moving only very slightly less than normal. As the same pace is maintained, this will result in an increase of the tempo of the hoof beats on the ground— obviously, therefore, the horse will bunch towards his centre, generating enormous power. Perfection in stride control will be the outcome of accurate and careful field dressage, of the rider's ability to size up a situation in a flash, and of his capability for translating his plan into the necessary action by the horse. There are three methods by which a stride can be authoritatively shortened. First by an increased tension from both hands, secondly by an increased tension with one hand, the other resisting in a

G*

supporting rôle, thirdly by bending the horse's head slightly from side to side towards the leading leg. For all three it is imperative that a strong leg is used to make certain that pace is maintained and that the hind quarters sweep forward and under. It is best therefore for the seat bones to be in contact with the saddle during the operation.

In the first and second methods care must be taken that the moment the shortening of one stride is completed, the feeling on the horse's mouth returns to normal. If two consecutive ones are shortened, then normal feeling must be resumed after the second. When the second method is adopted, the same hand should not always be used in the acting capacity, as the horse can acquire the habit of jumping crookedly towards the acting hand. The third is a method that the horse must learn as a separate lesson, and it should not be used during the last few strides before take-off. A horse unaccustomed to it can well think he is being asked to begin a change of direction. The amount shortened each time the head moves towards the leading leg will be small, but the method is artistic, and its effect useful, particularly when coming out of a wide curve. Whatever method is employed, the main consideration must be the maintenance of pace and of a constant head carriage. Outside the realm of dominance, the same shortening effect can be produced by suggestion in the last two or three strides before take-off. By ensuring that pace is kept uniform, by urging the hind quarters forward, and by holding the forehand back towards the centre, the rider can suggest to his horse that there is ample room for an extra short stride before take-off.

Gradually the horse will learn to accept the suggestion as sensible, and will treat it as a definite indication—but, if the rider's judgement has erred, his horse can still perform without the suggested extra stride. Shortening by firm suggestion can be invaluable when negotiating lines of related fences, and those of the staircase variety. Lengthening is, of course, the reverse of shortening. By increasing the overall measurement of one or two strides, the unwanted fraction beyond an even number can be absorbed into that number, with a resultant slight increase of pace. The difficulty lies in the fact that it is essential that the lengthening process is carried out with the hind quarters to the same extent, or slightly more, as the forehand. The spring must remain compressed. Any tendency towards elongation of the horse's body will

35. *The non-jumping stride within a double fence.*

36. *The non-jumping stride within a double fence in the process of lengthening.*

37. *The non-jumping stride within a double fence in the process of shortening.*

dissipate his propulsive power, and he will not be capable of making any height. To lengthen the stride the rider must be in an attitude of strength, with seat bones contacting the saddle. He must drive the hind quarters forward and, fractionally after, ease the feeling with his fingers to allow the whole horse to stretch, so increasing the length of that stride. Immediately upon completion, the feeling must return to normal. At no time must the rider's trunk move back from its usual position, and he must be in time and rhythm with the movement. Stride control provides finesse in the approach. When the controlling technique and the horse's training have reached top level, stride control should be barely perceptible, so that the whole performance is elegant, fluent and effective. Naturally the accuracy of the control becomes both more difficult and more necessary as the proximity of two fences grows smaller, culminating in a one non-jumping stride double.

DOUBLES OR COMBINATION FENCES

A double or combination fence is the most difficult type of test. Here endless practice and patience are essential both for the rider and the horse. Anything difficult needs reserves of impulsion. The rider must therefore accept an unwritten law that his approach to such fences, however simple they may appear, is always full of impulsion, and that his general attitude to the whole affair is bold, confident and resolute. It is essential to get out the other end! The rider's position and actions during each jump of a combination fence should be similar to those for an individual unrelated one, but his attitude from landing to take-off must differ, because he will require to be in a position of maximum strength during the one or two non-jumping strides. When his seat bones contact the saddle on landing, they must remain in contact until they automatically leave again at the next take-off (Plate 35). During this short period his aim must be to maintain balance and release impulsion as necessary—a sympathetic and elastic feeling on the mouth must be assured. When the inside distance is suitably free going, the horse's acquired system of moving off freely in his stride on landing will take him well on to the next take-off platform. But when the distance is either longer or shorter than that which suits the particular horse, the rider will have to take steps to dispose of the unwanted fraction.

For the majority of horses a long distance poses the bigger problem. In a one stride double it will mean that the whole of the unwanted fraction must be absorbed into the one existing stride—obviously this is a matter for the production of all available impulsion. The process must start with an attacking policy during the approach. As the hind legs come to the ground after the first jump, the rider must begin to exert strong leg pressure, and continue pushing until the next take-off. The hands must give in sympathy to allow the stride to be lengthened, normal feeling being regained fractionally before take-off. To be certain of making height and distance at the second jump, the spring must be kept compressed during the non-jumping stride (Plate 36). When the distance is shorter than suitable, the non-jumping stride has to be decreased in length. Impulsion will still be necessary to help the horse to bounce off the ground from a short stride. Hence the rider must restrict the extent of the forward stretch of the forehand during the stride away after landing, by increasing the feeling on the horse's mouth from the moment the fore feet touch the ground (Plate 37). He must, however, still push the hind quarters forward to obtain maximum compression and must return to normal feeling just before the next take-off. If the jump in is an upright, he can afford to stand away from it to obtain pitch, which in itself will help to shorten the stride. Similar procedures can, of course, be adopted for a two stride double. In a combination fence comprising a short distance followed by a long, the rider will need to maintain tremendous impulsion to make the final stretch. A bold and resolute approach, a high state of balance, great impulsion, and a spirit of attack, are all very vital factors in the negotiation of modern closely related fences.

WATER

It seems absurd that a horse should find any difficulty in jumping 14, or even 16, ft. of water. It would seem that all he has to do is simply step a little further! But it doesn't work out that way, and all over the world the water jump takes its toll. Mistakes made at water by a bold horse, who has learnt that height makes distance, are more often than not attributable to the rider. One often sees all the precepts of good approach work suddenly thrown to the winds, and the rider chancing his arm with unbalanced speed. A line from Bromley-Davenport's immortal poem 'The dream of the Old Meltonian' puts the matter in a nutshell. Coming down to take on the dread Whissendine, the dreamer's exhortation to his young thoroughbred horse aptly describes in two lines the preamble and the finish to the approach to water— 'With your muscular quarters beneath you collected, prepare for a rush like the Limited Mail' and then, '. . . with a quick shortened stride as the distance you measure'. Crescendo pace from not too far away, great power from behind, a firm acceptance of the bit, and a take-off platform as close as possible to the water, reached from a shortened stride, these must be the rider's objectives. Precision at water is just as important as it is for other fences— but it must be at real speed (Plate 38).

CHAPTER SIX

Inspection of the Course on Foot:
Bridles—Martingales—Nose Bands

Time after time the words 'Follow the chosen track' have been used in this book. The time has now come to go into details of when it can be chosen, and of the various factors that govern the actual choice.

Before the start of any jumping competition, competitors are given the opportunity to inspect the course on foot. In well-regulated shows ample time is given, it being realised that it is a matter of the utmost importance to riders. Before this, and at least 30 minutes before the starting time, however, a plan of the course should be prominently displayed in or near the Collecting Ring. This plan will provide valuable information. It will give the class number, its title, and the conditions under which it is judged. It will show the distance of the course, the speed per minute at which it is to be run, and the time allowed. It will give the fences used in the jump, or jumps-off, numerically, the distance of the jump-off course, the speed, and the time allowed. All this information will be tabulated. The plan itself, not necessarily to scale, depicts the start and finishing lines, the position of each fence in the course numbered in the order to be jumped, and so the rough route to be followed. Jumps comprising double or combination fences will be drawn separately, and marked a, b, or c as well as the fence's own numerical number (Figure 13). The type and size of the fences will not be shown. The route may be defined directionally by a solid line. If such a line is used it is obligatory to follow it. Failure to do so entails disqualification for taking the wrong course. All this information should be carefully digested. The way round the course can be learnt, so that there is no delay when the time for the inspection arrives. The design will show

CLASS 2.   TALLY HO STAKES   TABLE A3.

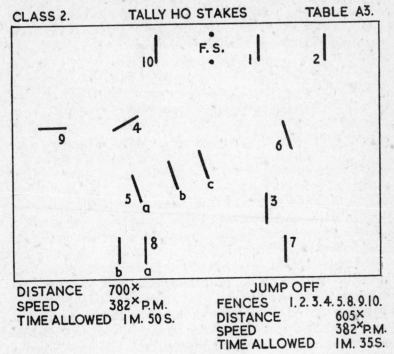

DISTANCE	700ˣ	JUMP OFF	
SPEED	382ˣ P.M.	FENCES	1. 2. 3. 4. 5. 8. 9. 10.
TIME ALLOWED	I M. 50 S.	DISTANCE	605ˣ
		SPEED	382ˣ P.M.
		TIME ALLOWED	I M. 35 S.

Fig. 13. Plan of a course

where difficult changes of direction can be expected—and, opti-
mistically, it will be as well to learn the jump-off course.

The walking of the course needs to be a routine matter, so that
every detail is dealt with progressively and quickly. Be ready then
to go into the arena as soon as allowed and, having learnt from
the plan the direction to take, start with a straightforward walk
round, checking the exact position of each fence, the angle at
which the fences are sited in relation to each other, and so the track
to be taken between them. Walk along this track. Note quickly
the type and structure of each, and the sequence of different types.
When fences are obviously, or closely, related, step the distances.
Memorise them or jot them down on paper. Do not go back
and check; this will be done later. Make a quick appraisal of
the going, and, having reached the finish, pause a moment or two
to make certain that the way round is clear and that the difficult
parts of the course have been spotted. Then start a second circuit,

which will be the detailed survey. Taking into account the type of each consecutive fence, the extent of changes of direction, and the angle of fences in relation to each other, walk exactly the track that is to be taken. Examine the going throughout, especially in the take-off zone of each fence. It may pay to jump towards a corner. Measure carefully again, by stepping, distances between related and closely related fences, thereby evolving a plan to cope with distances that do not suit exactly the particular horse or horses. The type, size, and structure of jumps comprising such fences will determine the pace required during the segment of the approach to them, and the amount of impulsion that will be necessary. Remember that a downhill gradient or hard going shortens a distance, and an uphill one or heavy going does the reverse. If a fence is sited soon after a sharp change of direction, pick the point where the straight portion of the approach will start, and so estimate the number of strides from there to take-off.

After a solitary, slow journey round the whole course from before the start to the finish, make a final check to ensure that following the right route will be automatic. In spite of all this, there may well be one or two tricky problems to which a solution is not clear. If this is so, ask for advice from an authoritative source, preferably one well acquainted with the particular horse. Finally, being brimful of confidence and a born optimist, check the jump-off course, with particular emphasis on ways and means of saving time. When the competition starts, provided that the order of jumping allows, watch good riders on good horses, who will give practical reassurance of the decisions made on foot in the arena. All this makes it very clear that it is essential for the rider to know exactly what his stepping measurements mean in relation to his horse's stride. I have often been asked by someone in a hurry—'What's the double like?' I have found that if I reply 'It's all right, measures eight' the inquirer is perfectly happy, apparently not realising that it is very doubtful if eight of my steps cover the same distance as eight of his! There can be no question that an intelligent and systematic routine for inspection will go far towards winning a prize.

BRIDLES

I do not propose to enter into a thesis on bitting, but there are two good kinds of bridle, and many that suit particular cases effectively. The two that give best service are the jointed snaffle and the double bridle. Each has various different patterns. The others are all of Pelham type, most of which can be used with either one or two reins. Before the last war a hunter in England was not considered to be properly turned out unless he wore a double bridle, but in Ireland the position was reversed, anything other than a snaffle being considered dangerous for bank jumping. Since then fashions in England have changed. The snaffle is now the almost universal bit, and indeed a great majority of post-war horsemen readily admit that they are not able to use two reins properly. This is a great pity. Specialised riding apart, many people who hunt, or ride only for pleasure, would find greater enjoyment were they to study and practise the use of a

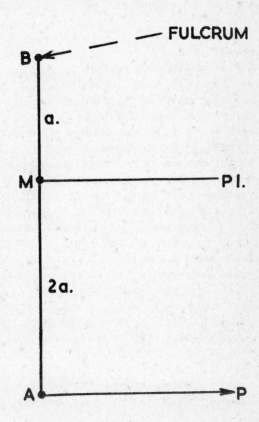

Fig. 14. The Second Order of Levers. The fulcrum is at B. A pull P produces action P1. Therefore P1=3P

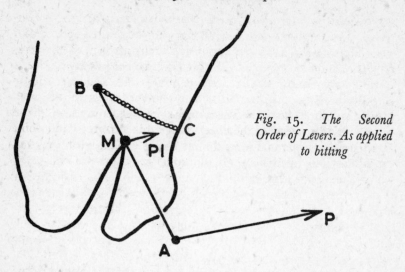

Fig. 15. *The Second Order of Levers. As applied to bitting*

double bridle. For show jumping a snaffle will be the best bit to use, always provided that implicit obedience and fluid balance can be produced and maintained.

For the early stages of training the snaffle will be the right one to choose. But it may not suffice to help towards good final results and, if not, the double bridle is the best type of curb bit to try because, having two separate mouthpieces retaining their own separate powers, its total result is a composite one provided by the normal snaffle action, and that of the curb bit, used singly or simultaneously. The delicate combination of the two will produce light and accurate shades of control. The jointed snaffle, or bridoon of a double bridle, should just touch the corners of the mouth without wrinkling them. If it lies too low there is a danger that the horse may get his tongue over and injure its roots. The curb is a lever action bit, the pressure transmitted to the horse's mouth being a multiple of the pressure exerted on the reins. The mouthpiece of the bit should be of a width that, when placed in the mouth, it fits close on to the outer surface of the lips without either pressing them or being subject to lateral displacement. The curb bit works according to what is technically termed the Second Order of Levers (Figure 14). With the fulcrum at B, a pull P produces action P1, so that P1 = 3P. P and P1 act in the same direction. Figure 15 applies this to bitting. The point

38. The water jump in the Piazza di Siena, Rome.

39. The late 'Sunsalve', ridden by David Broome at the White City; European Champions in 1961 and Individual Bronze Medallists at the Rome Olympic Games of 1960.

B is made the fulcrum by the curb chain. The pull P at A produces a pressure P1 on the bars of the horse's mouth. It is essential therefore that the double bridle is fitted according to this system. The bridoon is fitted as for a snaffle. The curb should be as low as possible in the mouth. The curb chain must lie, and stay, snugly in the curb groove. When pull P is given with the rein, the curb chain must act just before the mouthpiece begins to slide up the mouth, thus preventing the cheeks of the bit moving round point B, where the upper end joins the bit head stall. Fitted in this way the curb chain and the mouthpiece of the bit always act in the same places.

MARTINGALES

Martingales are purely and simply artificial aids, and fall into the same category as whips, spurs, stirrup irons and leathers and, indeed, saddles. It is perfectly possible to ride without any of them! The most valuable part of the martingale is the neck strap. I consider it to be my lifeline, and have often thought how much happier the lot of many horses would be were their owners to have a neck strap to hook a finger under in moments of distress! I find it impossible to understand why this practice should ever be considered *infra dig*. However, an ordinarily fitted running martingale has no positive action, and a loose standing one only prevents a horse from suddenly throwing his head very high.

NOSE BANDS

Periodically the drop noseband crops up as the subject for controversial correspondence. It is just another item on the list of artificial aids. When properly fitted it serves to prevent the horse from opening his mouth or crossing his jaw to an extent that will make it possible for him to evade the proper action of the bit.

Artificial aids are man's inventions to assist him towards perfection in horsemanship. If used with discretion, tact, and knowledge, there can be no good reason why such things should not be welcomed, and made use of as required.

PART TWO

CHAPTER SEVEN

Conclusion

Much has been written on the subject of the horse. Until the invention of the internal combustion engine everyday life revolved in large measure round him; as a beast of burden and a means of transport he was indispensable. He became the central figure in many sporting activities—and, significantly, he became part of English domestic life. Now, when he is used almost only in the realm of sport, he always attracts attention, and the majority of people have affection for him as a species and as an instrument of entertainment. The specialised horseman is closer to him than others, for he has to study the horse's character, and make an assessment of the best means of developing it to his own ends. As long ago as 400 B.C. Xenophon wrote that 'fair things by toil are won', which has always been a truism. It is, however, the methods and usages making up the toil that really count. Man must certainly be the master, and supremacy presupposes domination. The degree of domination imposed in show jumping varies considerably. 'All power corrupts, absolute power corrupts absolutely' Lord Acton thought, but it cannot be said that it applies to the power exercised by the horseman if he uses this power expertly and wisely. Forcible methods may break a horse's spirit, and domination can be complete—but the cost may be high.

The horse is a freedom-loving animal. His natural liberty is a blessing, and it is a tremendous asset when he is asked to jump big and difficult fences. Courage, initiative and enjoyment go hand in hand with a sense of liberty, and if a horse knows that his liberty will not be restricted he will co-operate cheerfully with his rider's wishes, will have confidence in his decisions, and will become entirely obedient. If, on the other hand, all his natural instincts and impulses are regimented, and thus repressed, he may well become an automaton without character and ambition, and may respond only through fear. Results may be obtained, but will produce no confidence or happiness. I do not like a situation of that kind. The horse is a friendly, trusting and courageous animal, deserving respect and admiration (Plate 39). Results can be obtained just as easily by tact, kindness and persuasion, and a horse receiving them will give cheerfully of his best and without question. Let him enjoy himself, therefore, as we enjoy him. Let him savour the thrills and excitements of life as he gives us pleasure.

Events and new inventions move with the times, some for better, and some no doubt for worse. The horse world follows much the same pattern. We have our own particular and favourite sports. Some are racing enthusiasts, others delight in show jumping or three-day events, and a few are followers of the high school. But behind all of them is the backbone of British riding— fox-hunting. The sport of our ancestors is still so much part of English country life. It has had its ups and downs, and in this modern age has much to contend with, but the difficulties and frustrations are more than worth while. The thrills and the benefits to man and horse will always be there,

> *So give me the brave wind blowing,*
> *The open fields and free,*
> *The tide of the scarlet flowing,*
> *And a good horse under me—*
> *And give me that best of bounties,*
> *A gleam of November sun,*
> *The far spread English counties,*
> *And a stout red fox to run.*

Index